MW00561342

# A BEGINNER'S GUIDE TO CREATING REALITY:

## AN INTRODUCTION TO RAMTHA AND HIS TEACHINGS

JZK Publishing™

# A BEGINNER'S GUIDE TO CREATING REALITY:
## AN INTRODUCTION TO RAMTHA AND HIS TEACHINGS
© 1997 JZK, Inc.

ISBN: 1-57873-025-2

Published by:
JZK Publishing ™
PO Box 1210
Yelm, WA 98597
(360) 458-5201
Fax (360) 458-2183
email: greg@ramtha.com
http://www.ramtha.com

Cover Art & Design by Guustaaf Damave
Layout Design by Greg Simmons
Cover Layout by Brett Alt

Other Titles by JZK Publishing:
The Mystery of Love (audio/book)
The Mystery of Love (CD/book)
The Plane of Bliss

# ACKNOWLEDGMENTS

First and foremost, I want to acknowledge Ramtha the Enlightened One for the  profound spiritual wisdom and love he has given all of us who have been his students so that this work could come into fruition.

To the students of RSE, both national and international, who have applied these marvelous truths in their lives, radiantly affecting the lives of many.

To my beautiful staff and all the people who worked on this book, especially Greg Simmons (editing and layout), Debbie Christie (editing), Pat Richker (proofreading), Brett Alt (cover layout), Melissa Peizer, Gary Craig, and Don Marshall for their work on the illustrations.

To Dr. J. Gordon Melton for his exhaustive research and counsel and for his fight for religious freedom all over the world.

To the wonderful people of the Yelm community.

-JZ Knight

# A BEGINNER'S GUIDE TO CREATING REALITY:

## AN INTRODUCTION TO RAMTHA AND HIS TEACHINGS

## Table of Contents

## Introduction
### by JZ Knight

# Introduction

Know yourself and you will know the universe and the Gods
(Inscription in the Temple of Delphi)

**Dear Reader:**

The following book is based on the concept of an ancient mystery school brought into the close of the twentieth century, an age which wallows in alarming materialism, where neither the church imprisoned by its own dogma and political intrigues nor science locked within the confines of matter know how to make individuals whole. Science need not change its methods, only broaden its scope, and religion need not change its traditions but rather remember its origins: the Spirit and its primal significance. The restoration of the link between the visible and the invisible, for the useful application of the omnipotent in our everyday lives, becomes the new conscious bridge to traverse the abyss that separates heaven from earth. Such a labor is called the Great Work. The concept of Ramtha's Ancient School of Wisdom is one whose academy is being built as each initiate/ student becomes the individual building stone.

At the heart of the mystery school is what Ramtha refers to as "the Void: one vast nothing materially, yet all things potentially," and Pythagoras referred to as "the Absolute." This is the essence of the uncreated being, the un-created God, the nothing from which all potentials spring. The Void is the great nonmanifest from which the ephemeral worlds are made manifest. As the manifest worlds change and eventually pass away, the Void remains unchanged. This eternal essence has been concealed from humanity, for man only perceives the things of tangible form, not knowing that these forms are combined with the infinite. Is it then possible for humanity to know what is concealed from them or, as Pythagoras asked, "Has anyone

7

ever seen the master of time, the soul of the suns, the source of intelligence?"

Ramtha teaches that one cannot see the Void or see the unchangeable, for to do so would declare a separateness from that which we ineffably are. We can only become one with it and in this way define a relationship that results in the bestowing of dimension, intelligence, and essence to things of form. It is precisely this divine relationship that God as moving Spirit is thus defined. We, humanity, are the Gods that bring the harmony that exists between what is seen and not seen. When becoming or being the Void, the student can begin to fathom this center of all things and in this the Great Work begins. The student undergoes initiations that bring closer the divine relationship by resembling the Gods that work the fires of creation. The work of the school is the combining of the scientific knowledge with the esoteric understanding of Spirit, coupled with the mastery of things through will, thus mastering the personal storms that divide the individual against the unity that manifests God as self.

Ramtha refers to us as the "forgotten Gods," an appropriate statement considering what most consider God to be — a magnificence that created humanity but remains apart and distant from them — thus forgetting our own divine origins and activities which have themselves defined the term "God." Gods did not preexist all else, but rather the Void was first, eternal, and absolute. The Void through an unimaginable contemplation created a principal point, which Ramtha refers to as Point Zero. This point contained Consciousness and Energy potentially and was the child of the Void. Point Zero was an indivisible substance which contained infinite Consciousness and Energy, the primal fire that would form the engines of creation. This is the Spirit, the essence of everything, and it is this essence which constitutes the definition of God as ourselves. We the Spirit are the first principle embodying divine faculties. The metaphor of the mystic lotus can help us understand this more clearly. Imagine for a moment an Egyptian initiate, lying in his sepulcher, who sees emerging from the blackness of a starless night a brilliant point of light. The point slowly begins to open like a radiating flower with its incandescent center unfolding and spreading out like a rose of brilliant light with a thousand petals. We are the flower unfolding from the source. From that moment God is manifest — we, you, I. From that moment we too contemplated and doubled the self into divisible substance. We now possess the active ingredient of Consciousness and Energy, represented in the ancient schools of thought as the eternal masculine (Consciousness) and the eternal feminine (Energy). Thus this perfect union of Consciousness and Energy forms the perfect union of generative and reproductive faculty which later would generate the world and the essence of God as indeed ourselves. It is this union that is responsible for the unfolding of God in time, dimension, and space.

God as ourselves can now be defined as the human being, a body garment worn by God as Spirit for the purpose of making known the unknown in the physicality of the three-dimensional world. The soul of man records this progress in holographic energy forms as a log of the journey. This blending of body as garment, soul as memory, and Spirit as God working in distinct harmony is what facilitates the creation of reality. The knowledge of these is the actual key to life from the constitution of the cell to the hyperphysical constitution of humanity as God. The triad of the threefold nature of body, soul, and Spirit produces the phenomena we refer to as the mind of man which constructs thought forms around which energy is patterned, creating the fluid of cosmic reality. Humanity alone is responsible for evolving matter held in earthly roots for the purpose of experiencing these in physicality and bringing forth all potentials from the Void into a knowable experience. These creative thoughts bring worlds into evolution, removing veil after veil from the process of divinity itself.

—JZ Knight

# I.

# Ramtha: An Autobiography

O ver the years Ramtha has spoken on many occasions about his sojourn into embodied life many centuries ago. Below is a selection of stories which introduce Ramtha as the very human person who lived much as each of us and yet who rose above his mundane condition to be the Enlightened One, not one to be worshipped but as the first among many masters who remembers their origin and seeks to become like Ramtha. Some of these stories were told in answer to specific questions asked of him by various students.

I am Ramtha the Enlightened One. I was known as Ram. Why, say you, I was known as Ram? Because when I was anointed upon a great mount I was called the Ram who comes from the mount into the valleys. I did not besiege kingdoms. I let them besiege themselves.

Prepare yourself. We shall speak evenly.

There were times in my obedience, in my learning, that I was a waif of sorts. I was tender in my frailties of my bodily movement. I had not strength to bring in the kindling for the brazier. Why was I this way? For I had not that which is nourishment to eat. I had not that which is called linens and furs to warm me when the winter and the silence of the whiteness came forth. I had not these things, thus I was withered in bodily form.

But grave upon my being was that of my motheren's being. For weakened so was she that to the infant that sucked at her tender breast there was no milk, for she had starved. And my sistern that was suckling at my mother's breast was very weak. Why, say you, we have this in our life? For we are the peasants, we are the nonessentials, we are the no-entities of a governed land.

Who governed this land? Those of means who had all of us live about their lands and run their fields and say they would not grant us even a stalk for our own living. And what, say you, did they with these things? They locked them into granaries. They fed themselves with fastidious fingers leaving the rest of us to starve.

I say unto you this was unjustness. And who be this God they have spoken of? I am angered, for my mother weeps for there is no milk in her breasts. I run from that of my hovel, and there be a great mountain in a distance I barely see and my journey hath been of ninety days. Ninety days of devouring locusts and roots and urnments of ants did I found this mountain. For if be he God, he would live there above all of us as those who governed our land lived above us. And lo I sought him out. Yet he was not there, except the cold. And I wept heartily until the whiteness iced itself from my tears.

"I am a man. Why have I not the dignity of one?" And behold there came unto me a sweet maiden as you have not seen, whose gilded hair danced around her. The crown that be upon her hair was not of lilies or of rosebuds or of irises but an unknown flower. Her draperies, indeed her gowns, were translucent and mellow and free, and behold she came unto me and gave me a great sword that sang. It sang. Yet it took nigh nine hands to hold its handle, it was so great.

She gave it unto me and she said, "Oh, Ram, oh, Ram, I beseech you, you who have learned and broken our Spirit into pity. It is true there must be a truth that lingers in the land, and thus your prayer has been heard. You who will be a man of means and conviction take you this sword and wear it well." And she was gone with herself.

I was blinded in my madness and my illusions by what I had seen. No longer did I shiver against the great cold, for I found warmth there. And thus when I looked again where my tears had iced themselves, there grew a flower of such sweet refrain and color that I knew the flower would be that what is termed hope.

I came down from the mount with my great sword to the hovel of my mother who had perished with the child who was suckling upon her breast. I burned my mother and my sister upon a funeral fire, and I wept. No longer weak of bodily movement or frail, I became a Ram in all the sense of the word and made war upon the tyrants of all my peoples who were enslaved by them. And my army brought justice into the land and to all the lands we marched upon. And of the flowers, wherever we trod they grew freely.

Student: *I wanted to ask some questions about you. I believe that you've only had one expression upon this plane. Am I correct in that? I think through the understanding of your life and experiences, I hope to learn greater about myself. And I'm curious as to what were your experiences. What brought you to creating your body on this plane? You once told us about Buddha's experiences. Why did you come here? I guess what I'm trying to ask is what drives any God to create the body and to live out his experiences and find his way back?*

I did not create my body. I was left with that which is called the Atrium of the Constants. The Atrium of the Constants was a shelf. It was called the Mantle of Terra. On the Mantle of Terra, after the five races had made their descent upon the plane, I was one that had not descended into the planes. There was a whole mass that was with me. It was not unusual.

For who was going to be there, master, when copulation began to stir itself and the fruitful seed began? What soul and Spirit were going to inhabit the seed if God had split himself into the two in order to make an extension of himself into creativity for his beloved brethren? He would not become the other brethren that he created from the two; he could not. The child that is created from the two has to have a soul and Spirit. Bodies are easily made. Souls and Spirits are forever. It was through a bodily movement that I desired to come through to express.

I had been in many ways a foolhardy God, as all were foolhardy Gods in our beginnings and misused our thoughts and our understandings to a competitiveness that destroyed a wondrous place. And I was amongst them, as you were amongst them.

And why do we want to express in the things that we create? If we do not express into the reality, how know we the reality exists? How know we the creativity of what we've done has an existence until we have become a part of it?

And when the races of man were blooming and fostering unto itself life and culture and love and exuberance of God loving himself, it was in a natural order of events that I had my choice to come, as all in the Mantle of the Atrium did. And I chose to come. I favored Terra, you see. I favored Terra, for Terra was a hope to us. It was beautiful, luminous, virtuous, and we had learned from our erroneous errors of our past and I wished to be a participant in it.

You see, what I did not know is that once you lower your vibrations to yet lower fields, you forget the higher fields for you are living in the lower. When anyone is born from the Atrium onto this plane, they forgot the higher. It was in their instincts. As animals have their instincts, man has them also but not in complete memory as it were. The moment that Spirit takes in rapture the completeness of the body, Spirit has the totality of memory but ego does not.

Thus when being upon this plane, I was born an ignorant barbarian. You see, how could I comprehend the ignorance and the separation of species, whether one be a barbarian or whether one be a king? How would I know what the difference of those attitudes were? For me, I could not define them for I had not been them.

You see, higher elements never judge lower elements. Only lower elements judge the higher because the higher has not the capacity to understand the lower element, for it is not the lower element. You understand what I say? Before I entered I did not understand that man was enslaved to man. I did not understand a waste called human life, deprivation, enslavement. How could I understand those things? I was not those things, you see. And it wasn't until I became who I was was I at the mercy of being ignorant, being a barbarian, a soulless, mindless dog. You see, that was what we were considered. How did I know that that meant that I was to be lower than the aristocracy that was called *Atlanteans* * until I had been the victim of it?

When you are ignorant and you do not possess the common intellect of the land, then you are riding on the outskirts of a society that does not accept you, for if they do, it reminds them perhaps of their own failing, you see. Ego does not like that. *Altered* ego does not like to be reminded it is altered.

In not having the privilege of education and that which is called the sciences, not having the privilege to express as a human being, it was nigh out of hate and pain and unexplainable hurt and despair and sorrow that I had nothing else to challenge, except perhaps the reasoning that brought me here. I did not know at that time that I was the reasoning that brought myself here. You see? But out of that learning, I could comprehend an element that I found more forceful than man, an element I found much more intelligent than man, an element that I found could live in peaceful coexistence beside and in spite of man. I assertained it must be the Unknown God.

And it was these elements of nature, dear entity, that taught me, you see. And I'm very fortunate for being taught by the elements and reasoning with them; I had none to say that I was wrong. And the elements never taught me failure, you see, because they're consistent. That is how I learned.

I learned from something that is consistent, that is never failing, that is

---

* Ramtha from time to time coins words to make a point or to emphacize his teaching. These words are in *italics* throughout these writings.

easily understood if man puts his mind to it. And because of that I was not at the hands of the hypocrisy of dogma or superstitious belief or multifaceted Gods that you're trying to please, or the stigma that perhaps we were lower in perfection and could never obtain it. I was never at the hands of that kind of teaching. That is why it was easier for me to do in my one existence what it has taken many a millennia to do because they have looked for God in another man's understanding. They have looked for God in governmental rules, in church rules, in history, that they never even question who wrote it and why they wrote it. They have based their belief, their understanding, their life, their thought processes on something that life after life after life has proven itself a failure. And yet man stumbling in his altered ego, afraid to admit to himself that perhaps he has erred, continues the steadfast hypocrisy that only leads to death.

I was a most fortunate entity. The sun never cursed me and the moon never said I must be this way. The wind teased me and tantalized me, and I was tantalized by the frost and the dew and the smell of grass and insects going to and fro and the cry of a night hawk; you know, they are unfailing things. Their science is simple. And the wonderful thing about them I learned, entity, is that in their steadfastness they utter not one word. The sun did not look down at me and say, "Ramtha, you must worship me in order to know me." And the sun did not look down at me and say to me, "Ramtha, it is time to wake up and look upon my beauty." It was there when I saw it, you see.

That is the beginning. That will never fail you. That will teach you cleaner, clearer truth than anything ever written by man.


Ramtha: What say you?

Student : *I would like you to tell me of the past life that I had when I knew you.*

Ramtha: How know you, master, that you knew me?

Student: *I just had a feeling that I did.*

Ramtha: I will tell you.

There came the tenth year of our march. We came into a valley of some renowned fame. The valley had always been peaceful with its peoples, and there be no tribes that maraud and put forth tyranny and fear upon the land.

There came what is termed a diplomat of sorts that met our march outside of the valley of Nizire. We had set forth an encampment and had been in our camp and settled in what is called nigh three months in your time. The women were busy in their affairs, and all entities that prepare for an encampment, master, are continuing and sustaining life and caring for flocks and herds that follow the entourage.

There came forth in a stormy afternoon, master, with the passing of great thunder and lightening, a runner of noble distinction. He came forth and brought forth a litter of sorts. And all the Nubians who brought forth the litter, great was their stature, and they were wetted by the cooling rains and the ominous thunder. They had still, even the hour they approached the encampment, the waters running from their ebony bodies unto that which is called the saffron sand.

And they appeared to take from their burden and to place it on the ground and to pull forth the most elegant drape to permit a statesman of some notoriety in the land of Nizire to come forth. A Nubian that led the front march of this entourage, master, hailed that all should tend to themselves of the arrival of this entity who had good tidings for the march and the hour of the Ram.

I cursed the entity and despised his litter and the fact that he put forth his pompous being upon softened cushions and had gentle and kind men care for him. For in those times I loved not the God of my being but hated and was angered by all things, for tyranny had taken from me the motheren of my being, the sistern of my being, and the beauty of my being.

The entity was not met by me in my countenance but was seen to enter what is called my awning. And I made him wait. As soon, with tedious impatientness, as he voiced his impertinence at this unkindness and unfairness was it that the Ram was presented unto him.

The Ram comes forth and the entity begins to proclaim that the Ram and the host of the Ram had been invited into the palace of Nabore in the valley of Nizire to be the guest of a great council that had assembled to prepare treaties of sorts, that the land would not be tormented and burned and perished under by the terrible day of the Ram and his armies.

Now upon this I quickened in favor and gave unto him my cartouche to return unto his noble host. I told him that I would prepare a suitable entourage and would prepare my time to meet with him in what is called three days in their time. And thus it was.

L et me give you some description of the palace of Nabore. As you approach it you cross a riverbed of sorts that was not alive with rushing waters. But the smallest of water trickles down stone from stone and passes into some forgotten pit that issues forth from the other side of a small mountain. And as we approach the palace, master, behold if you stand forth and look to the northeast on the other side of the river you will see what is called the Ptolemy. It is a great mound.

And there be a great fortress standing before us, ominous and awesome and beautiful. The stone is of a dull granite and does not have the lightness of beauty and color and takes on whatever the ages have given unto it, all stained and different colors. The gates are bronzed. In this time, master, the black metals, as they are so termed in your time, had not been finished upon the land as they are now. And all objects requiring strength were bronzed. The doors were bronzed and they were great in their gates. And amongst the towers that overlooked the fortress, master, there were great banners. The banners were silken beauties and all colors. And trumpets sounded as the entourage of the Ram approached on the other side of the small and insignificant river.

Behold as we worked ourselves up a desolate land, and I saw how no thing grew and became flourished in it. I began to question how this place could sustain in this barren wilderness.

The doors of the mighty gates, they do open. And behold my company, master, goes forward. And we are met by what is termed "dandies" in your time. They are not the lovers of women; they are the lovers of their own kind. They are trusted by the head of the palace of Nabore and will not forsake him. And they come forth, master, indeed and find us in great favor.

They take us forth quickly behind the doors, and there are women of foreign beauty as I have never seen that are lightly clothed but heavily decored in what is called brass and bronze and jewels and stones. And they found their delight in substance.

The gardens, they are wonderful. They perfume the air within the gates of Nabore. And there are fountains that issue forth water that are scented with jasmines and lilies and rose flowers. And they have trees that they have burnished and polished their trunks, as it were, that when the hand is put upon them they encounter that which is called the smoothness of bark. The leaves, they are green and supple, and the blossoms, they do flourish. It is most peculiar.

And looking upon you do not find a simple road, master, but a floor that is the whitest granite marble that I have ever seen. It is so white, master, that I have not even seen snows in high lands that compare to it. It is all clean and pure. Well, I marvel at this. We put forward our feet upon it and it cools them immediately. There is rest and comfort in this refuge in the middle of this wilderness in the valley of Nizire.

We are taken and ushered past gardens that loom with the procession of foreign flowers outside of the gate in what is called purple and white and rose and music and soft voices and faint voices of untold stories that go on behind the walls and gardens that lie therein. And women of such beauty, master, they attend all that is in my complement, and yet they all seem the same.

We are told that our quarters are prepared for us. We all shared the same quarters, for we would not be separate. And behold there are paintings and friezes that yet within one room after another, master, are greater than the one that we left before. And in the one great room that we occupy, it is all an open terrace into a lush and fertile garden. And there is a pool with strange fishes. And there are cushions and vases and alabaster jars and scented unguents and paintings and friezes on walls that depict battles unknown unto my countenance. And there are servants that are mute and deaf and know no thing except to serve, that are naked except the collar they wear around their necks and who are pleased to serve.

There is a small table inlaid with what is called pearl and made of lemon wood, a bounty of wine that is lovely and scented, and fruit and dates and meats. There are good foods there for us to eat. And immediately the comfort that we have not known is partaken of. And it is strange to watch the deaf and mute entities that wait on us. How know they that we are in desire? They never leave our company and watch all things that we do.

If you go from this splendid room unto the colonnaded garden, you would find statues, and they are not of animals or of God, as it were, but of people who all look the same. They are all beautiful, master. None is different. You will find the sweetness and the lushness of the garden, and the breezes were kind upon our countenance.

When the evening begins to fall upon the land, lanterns are lit and torches in the garden. And the light placates the mystery of this beautiful place which is shrouded in mystery and tempts us in desire. There came a'calling an esteemed runner to tell us that our audience has been prepared. We are refreshed. We are clean. We are given a clean linen, a kilt to put upon our beings, and leave and are ushered forth down a long corridor where it immediately has great and massive vases with sprigs of flowers on trees that I had seen in my garden, all alive.

We entered into what is called an anteroom before the great guard. And there awaits, master, a most peculiar mute entity. He is small in his character. His hair is bleached like the sun is bleached. His eyes dance with a warm fire, and he is muscular into his being and I presume him to be an athlete, a seeker to sports. And he asked for me, master, with a hand for the parting of my sword. It is not given that we should enter this sacred place armed. I give the mute my sword. And he takes it and looks upon it with a most grand style and considers it a treasure.

And once the doors are opened, I am permitted to go in and that of my following is not permitted. So in the reasoning of what is called preliminary talks, as you so term them in your times, master, I came in. And behold I saw men that were anointed and scented and adorned in all conceivable specter of color of gems and gilded to their very sandals in gold. They have surely not known the wilderness and all its effects. And I despise them, for they rot in their own cleanliness. And surely there are sufferers in this palace that must be at the hand of their own doing, that none speak, master, that all obey. And they bid me to come in. Their number is four.

As I approach, I hear the clouded and silken tongues begin to tell me how great my army is and how they desire and wish my encampment to draw closer into their valley, master, and unto their palace and how hopefully their culture with our esteemed force could bring together an awesome power. And I said no thing. And then when one would be so declarative as to call the gathering and the enormous force "heathens," master, I spat upon him and called him a pig.

The entity had fiery hate that flashed forth from his eyes and they moved from me. And there came up from my rear guard, master, unattended a most forceful entity with a great sword and runs me through.

To feel a blade penetrate the back of your being and to break the rib, puncturing from the back, and to sever what is called the passage and lungs and cleave this side of what is called the stomach, master, and to find its point bulging what is called the softness of your area in the front of your countenance, master, and to feel the hotness of your being exhilarated through the metal that now lies between you, master, is an unforgettable experience.

I had been run through.

The entity who was so skillful with his work with the sword hath put it forth and pushed it further, that the hilt of his sword lay even with my back and then pulled it out, master.

There is a falling. And I look upon the floor and it comes to me slowly. And as I come onto the floor I can see the discrepancies in the white marble that are hued towards the color of gray. And as I came unto the floor my face strikes the cold marble that had no warmth. And as I lay unable to see from the right side of my face and unable to speak, for my mouth is implanted upon the smooth, cold, relentless surface, there are things that call deep within me. And I begin to see a scarlet river as it ebbs and flows from my being. I see a crack in what seemingly was a perfect floor, master. And I watch as this scarlet ebbs to the floor, master, and drips to the crevice.

It is life; it is life that flows from me. What of the woman that I loved? She is no longer in life. What of the mother that I loved? She is no longer in life. What of a caress of a sweet woman? I would never know it. And of the children of my seed, had they been bastardized and been neglected? What of the great tree that I harkened unto at the times when hunger ravished my being? And where lies the mount now that once presented itself to me as a home? I will not see it again.

And I hear the echoing sound resounding in my being, master. And it begins to appear in the back of my throat, the hot river of life coming forth, and it spattered within my mouth. And what of I? I had been a ruthless entity that hated tyranny and despised despicable men who enslave others. It is the end of my days.

As I watch the blood issue forth from my being, master, there is a voice. It did speak unto me saying, "Stand up." It said unto me, "Stand up." I began to pull under me the knees of my being. And when doing so I heard the empty scabbard on my being strike the floor and scrape against it. And I put forth my palms and pulled up my head and raised my countenance, master, that my head was erect and even, and pulled up my left foot and stabilized it and put my hands upon my knee, not seeing the wound, and standing up.

There is a spitting of blood; it is issuing forth from my mouth, master. And the entity that ran me through dropped his sword and grabbed forth his amulet that dangled from around his neck, master, and fled. And the men with curled beards and anointed heads and skin and countenance, who first thought me to be immortal, master, have now seen that I am and they do flee.

And behold by gathering all the strength of being and holding my wound, as all of the river of its blood issues forth from my fingers and runs down the legs of my being, master, there comes forth the mute man who be outside of the door who had asked for my sword, and, seeing the Ram standing forth, begged at his feet for mercy. Though I could not speak, he pleaded for mercy; it was given. For how could I have possibly the strength to condemn this man who had asked for forgiveness when I am gaping through the belly of my being and my entrails are beginning to show?

I spoke to this being and asked him to go forth into my encampment and seek forth that entity that is called Gustavian Monoculus and an entity called Cathay and bring them to me. The entity went forth himself and harkened unto his being and ran away from me, master, only to return shortly to give me my sword and left.

If you put forth your fist and grab your being where you are wounded and clench it tightly, master, it ceases dying. That is what I did.

Behold there came forth Gustavian Monoculus and the entity called Cathay and I tell them to render perfect and to lay bare the kingdom, and they did so. And they returned me to what is called the Legion of Women that followed the procession of our march. And through women, master, and their gentle care and loving kindness did they tender to me, master, perfect. Being helpless at the hands of a woman, master, who takes charge of your life, a man can see life in a different perspective.

I could not forget the voice, master, that made me stand forth and kept me from dying. And I sought to find the face of the voice. When I was healed from that which occurred, master, I began to conquer and love that which I conquered; not all was laid bare but compromises were met, forgiveness was seen. And the softening of the Ram continued great into the march. I found the voice, master, when I found myself, the God that I was. I was the one who told me to stand up, master. The divine cause, the life, the principle, the understanding, the purpose, was me. With this

23

understanding, master, we changed the thinking of generations to come.

And who you had been unto me, master, was the mute entity that sent for and gave me my sword and brought back my complement. When all was laid bare in the palace of Nabore in the Valley of Nizire, you were not, master. You were cherished and suffered and tendered and became a part of my march and saw me ascend. Long did you grow in your years, past that which is called 120. Though you never spoke, master, for there was no tongue to speak with, your eyes and your thoughts and the presence of your being taught many. That is how you know me.

Student: *Thank you. That's the reason that I feel the way that I do towards you.*

Ramtha: It is a truth, master. And listen to me. Many peoples do not appreciate life or the small voice that speaks to them until they see it ebb from them. Blessed are all peoples who relish life and love it and abound in it and bless themselves for being participants in it. Learn?

Student: *I've learned.*

Ramtha: So be it.


Ramtha: Master, what say you?

Student: *Greetings, Ramtha.*

Ramtha: Indeed, greetings unto you.

Student: *I've made a discovery recently and that is that life can be fun. And as a matter of fact I think it's getting to be funner and funner.*

*I have a question. I ask myself "Why me?" and I get the answer, "Why not?" And I know you called me to you because I just came so easily. Why did you select me? Why did you select all of us rather than someone else?*

Ramtha: Why not?

Student: *There must be a greater reason than that. Is there?*

Ramtha: There is a greater reasoning, but it is nicer to say "Why not?"

Student: *I won't press you. That's fine. Another thing that I've been wondering about is ascension. I have heard that you said that you attempted ascension a number of times.*

Ramtha: Quite a number.

Student: *I wonder if you can tell me a little bit about what is involved, what it is actually what happened.*

Ramtha: When learning about the Source, I did not have a teacher to teach me in regards to the Source and the Father. It was an experience of simplicity that all take for granted, which is a good and proper term to be used in this society.

I learned from the weather. I learned from days. I learned from nights. I learned from tender and insignificant life that seem to abound in the face of destruction and war. The teacher unto my being was the Source.

When I contemplated the Father in all of His brilliance, there were two things that had me believe in life perpetual: the sun, which I called Ra, its advent of glory onto the horizons and its journey all through the heavens, ending up in the western sphere and passing into its sleep and permitting a wondrous beauty; the moon and her pale light to come dancing across the heavens to illuminate the darkness in mysterious and wonderful modes.

In spite of all of this I learned this also, that the mute voice of the Father and the son, though not reckoned with, controlled subtly life. All who were brave and gallant or warring with one another and planning debaucheries upon their favor ceased our debaucheries when the sun went down. And I saw an old woman pass from this plane, clasping heartily the crude woven linen that she had made for her son that had perished long ago. I saw her, master, pass in the light of the noonday sun. And her life ebbed from her body in shortened strokes, a'weeping. And I saw the old woman begin to shrivel in the light. And her mouth became drawn to open to an aghast expression, and eyes that gazed at the light untaunted. Nothing moved save the breeze in her old hair.

And I looked at the woman who gave birth to the son who perished; how great their intelligence was. And I looked up at the sun, who never perished. It was the same sun that the old woman saw when she first opened up her eyes in her mother's arms at birth coming through a crack in the ceiling. And it was the last thing she saw when she died.

And as we put away the old woman, I looked again at the sun and I reckoned with it. And I began to ponder it and days and life and creatures that lived in spite of man. And I began to reason that the Gods that are in man's mind are truly the personality of that which they feared and respected the most. And that the true God was one who permitted this illusion, this ideal, to come and go and still be there when they returned yet again another spring, another life.

Quickly I ascertained this, master, that it was that power, that life, that foreverness that is unceasingly there, that is where the true reverence, that the true God, the Unknown God, lies; life force.

When I found out who God was and what it was, through elevated thought, I did not wish to wither and die as the old woman had died. I had seen many gallant entities of my charge die, and I thought that there must be a better way to maintain as the sun maintains.

And behold as I was beginning to ponder in the state of mending in my direst despair of my body, once healed from it, I sat upon a solitary plateau and looked about far into yonder where there was a thick haze that slim outlines of ghostly mountains are seen and valleys yet uncharted. And I wondered how I could be a part of the essence that is the continuum.

Much to my surprise and great relief, there came a soft wind. And the wind took its pleasure upon me that hour. It wrapped itself and furled in my hair and through my fingers and dried the eyes that were tearing and caught up my cloak that was long and regal and whisked it over my head. Not a very noble position for a conqueror, you see. But as I uncovered my cloak over my head and put it down and shuffled myself back into proper study, the wind whirled beside me some saffron dust and made it into a soft column that went way into the sky. And I looked at the column.

That is when it occurred to me what the invisible power is all about. I contemplated the wind, master, and aligned myself with its elusiveness and lightness and contour that is indefinable. I contemplated the wind, and it was the wind that I became in my search for becoming.

The first occurrence did not occur until six years after my resurrection, as it were, and every evening, master, I would go upon a solitary place and gaze into the moon and her soft pallor and contemplate the wind.

And there came a time, much to my sweetness and surprise and my determinedness, that soon I found myself lofty in the heaven above myself. I did not know who I was when I turned to look back. But in a moment a realization occurred to me that I was further out than my simple speck of body that was upon the plateau. And I was feared. The moment I was feared, I opened my eyes and was again in the cold/hot sweat that a man can work himself into. I had been elsewhere outside of my prison.

I lowered myself, master, unto the ground and beckoned unto the Source, the power, the cause, the wind, and praised it for elevating me through its thoughts. And I never forgot its grace and its beauty and its bound for life that I had become that splendid moment.

And as I began to reckon at what gave me that elusiveness, it was complete, clear, determined thought that was aligned with an ideal, the wind. On the next eve I came unto my place of solitary movement. I contemplated the wind with exuberant joy. And I became no thing. And I went again and again. And I knew in reason that the experience was not a wishful imagination, but it had happened. I had seen a different perspective. I had been in the air as if I were a hawk. I had wings that I did not see. And I saw my pitiful self below me.

It was a long time, master, before I became the wind yet again. In reckoning in your time, two years from that event. And this event happened not on contemplating the wind but going into what is termed a restful sleep. I praised the Source, the sun, life, the saffron dust, the moon, the stars, sweet smells of jasmine; I praised it all. And as I closed my lids, behold I was in the heavens again. I was the wind.

It took a long time to reckon that once I was there how to go other places. And I steadfasted myself for long periods above myself tirelessly. And then it occurred to me that that which is termed the entity called

Cathay was in a most perilous position, as it were. For he, being a robust character that sought after the wondrous ways of women and strong drink and told stories that were made to be more than they were, merely to add the glamour to them, was caught up in a perilous position. I saw life ebbing from him from my viewpoint, master. And in order to go unto Cathay to relinquish his heel from the stirrup that strapped across the horse, the moment my thought was with him I was there, in the twinkling of an eye, and released the stirrup from his heel and stood over him and wished him well. He thought I was a dream.

I learned to travel in moments, that the conclusive God that aligned with the wind and the sun and the heavens was thought. For whatever thought is, the entity that is the God that you are is.

For many years I knew its passages into kingdoms and unto other entities and to lives yet unseen. I visited what is called civilizations in the birth of their future. I learned the ways of my beloved brethren who would follow me, master, in their advent on this plane to discover the Source.

You see, when you come here you do not have memory, for you are caught up in ego-self, pertaining to the body now. Once I learned these things, master, I began to teach the Source readily to all of my beloved brethren.

And then there came a day when it was time that this old man, master, his days were finished, that all that I had set out to accomplish, indeed who I was, was accomplished. I made my journey across a river termed Indus. And there on the side of the mountain called Indus, master, I communed with all my peoples. I bade unto them that this truth was a truth, that their divine guidance was not through me but the Source that had made me, as it had made them. Behold, for their belief and to their surprise, master, I elevated myself quite nicely above them. The women began to scream and were aghast, and the men who were soldiers were dropping their broadswords in wonderment. I saluted them farewell and to learn as I have learned, to become as I have become in their way.

When wanting to be whatever it is that you desire to be, align your thoughts with it. In the wind is a power that can intimidate a solitary soldier and take the earth and whisk it into the heavens in a single blow. And yet it cannot be harnessed or enslaved and it cannot be servant to anything save itself. I contemplated the free movement of the wind and became it. That is how.

Student: *That explains several things for me, as you well know. Thank you. I appreciate that.*

Ramtha: The difficulty that all have with this ideal is that they are still caught up in death and old age. And they are caught up in trying to find a machine that will get them there. And they are caught up in the complexities rather than the simplicity that the Father is. It is done simply; never arduously. So be it.

Student: *So be it.*


Student: *There is something I want to ask you. You've talked a lot about Atlantis to different people and you've spoken that you were there. You told us a story the last time we came to a workshop about creation, which was very beautiful, about where we all really came from. And I was wondering if you could tell this audience how Atlantis was formed and why it was destroyed and what it was like there and why you left. Could you tell us something about the history.*

Ramtha: Of the entirety of Atlantis, I was not a traveler upon it, only the most southernmost port which was called Onai. There was a canal, or a waterway as you would term it, that connected Atlantis with that which is called Mu. You understand what Mu means? Lemuria, the greatest motherland of all. Truly that was the cradle of civilization, if man wishes to find where it was.

But in the waterways, the pilgrimages that were making their advent to Atlantis at that time were doing so, for the land called Mu was overrun with the great beasts. They were remnants of a further creativity that have I explained to you in "Creation." And there were many peoples that had all their structures underground, you see. None in Lemuria had structures that were lived above the ground. They lived in that which is called a mount. There was only one mountain range, that be in the upper Pacific coast in this your country into that which is called the waterways. In that particular time they made their hovels in the mountains. But in the great flatlands, the great plain of Mu, all lived underground. Thus they had a wonderful network of tunnels, indeed highways and byways that were beneath the ground for the mere safety from the animals above. The animals became rampant, producing bigger and better, enormous creatures.

The entities that decided to stay with the motherland knew that the land was going to be going down, for the great waters were already beginning to form in the stratum. And when the land went down in its surface, it did so to the destruction of the animals and the beasts. And when it did, the continent shifted upon its rotating axis and gave unto the higher regions of Lemuria a great freeze. It was the freeze that finished them off.

It was that the land was going under. Those that were the old fathers of Lemuria chose to stay with their beloved land and go with it. They remember the time of their advent, you know. It is told in their history. The younger ones made their pilgrimage to Atlantis. And the one waterway that connected Atlantis unto Lemuria was a canal place.

We were called slaves, dogs, soulless, mindless. All that came from that continent were not loved and honored by the *Atlanteans*, for they were high in their intellect while the Lemurians were strong in the Spirit, the invisible understanding. My forefathers worshipped a power that they called the Unknown God. And even late unto your history, his name remained on altars throughout various civilizations.

When I came unto Atlantis, I came from a canal into the greatest port in Atlantis in its southern sphere called Onai. And you think this city (New York) to be great? Onai's port land would have made two of this city, along with its coast; it was enormous.

The bowl, or what they called a bowl, that separated the *Atlanteans* from the Lemurians, was a rather small barrier and it bowled in the center;

thus it had some waters within it. But the swampland was a most immobile place. Not even that which is termed outlaws by my beloved physician would tread into what is now called your America. And it separated the two continents in understanding.

Atlantis at that time was a continent of a civilization that had perfected the thought into the power of pure energy. They worshipped the intellect. That is why in this part of your country, in this that you call your Americas, that that of the eastern coastline is known for its intellect and that of the western is known for its Spirit. It is a truth. It is a lingering attitude that is here. The very coastline of your great city here (New York) indeed was a coastline of even farther islands of the northern part of Atlantis. Thus that which you call the Americas, Brazil, South America, they used to be like this. They were one land mass. And they formed into a point and where the point formed, all the land that went up from that was the greater continent called Atlantis. And what separated Atlantis from these two land masses was the canal zone that connected Lemuria to it. It was a singular waterway. It was the only port that the southern sphere of the north, Onai, had.

Now you say, "Where, Ramtha, were all of the waters, the oceans that we have?" They were still in your stratum. The water had always been in your stratum. That is what made the wondrous child called Terra fertile, for it took the sunlight and evenly deposited it all over the earth.

How did the freeze come about in the final days? The waters came down to the great waterway. When light had been perfected by the *Atlanteans* for travel, for the purpose of destruction, for the purpose of transmuting thoughts and things, a war broke out between a faction located on one of the moons and those of the continent. Those *Atlanteans* on the earth fired a light projectile at the moon, breaking and evaporating the stratum. The great light severed the great waterway in the stratum, and it was there that the water began to fall from the atmosphere in what you would term moisture.

Little bit by little bit as this was done, that which is called Lemuria began to rumble in its bowels and quake. And as it began to quake, the stratum that had been pierced by the great light began to flood Lemuria with water. As the water came down on the Lemurians, the earth began to tilt. For it is like when the babe is in the womb. If you puncture the womb, the water that is in the womb that protects the babe will throw the babe to one side, for the babe is balanced in the womb according to the water. It is the same as it is with Terra.

When the waters came down on the great planet, the planet shifted to the point of a great coldness. When it shifted and the hole was in the stratum, the sunlight was taken and condensed all around where the stratum still was and there was no warmth coming through the punctured hole, thus creating the great freeze.

It was all immaculately done, for it destroyed Lemuria, who were termed dogs, indeed no things, and all of the animals which were beginning to pose a threat to the *Atlanteans*.

Now what happened to Atlantis when the great tumbling and catastrophe of Lemuria began to fall? It began to fall in sections. It was the northern part of Lemuria that went first. And when it went under from the freeze, the waterways came and began to fill in each part as the continent began to shelve itself lower. As it began to do this, the continents that set themselves together as the supportive elements of Atlantis began to move apart. For the water came in through the waterway and began to cleave a waterway that separated the continents and they began to move. The continents of Brazil and .South America that were once together are now where a great waterway flows.

You see, the *Atlanteans* fervently believed that this was an act of their intelligence, for they were world conquerors. For their terrible light was not terrible at all. It was merely lasers, but in a more refined, useable state. They of themselves despised the pilgrims who had no intellect for machines. Once they saw the crumbling from afar and saw the stratum splitting, they were so arrogant to believe that their annihilation would never be and that the hole in the stratum was only an adventure to them.

The continent of Atlantis — it was referred to as *Atlantean* — it is and was the red civilization. What you term your Indians, your red people, are indeed the ancients known as *Atlanteans*.

Now during my time when the pilgrimage was set and there would be slums in Onai, it took a long time from this that I have told you to take into proper operation. The time from the first stratum pierce and to the canal raising itself and splitting itself took 600 years in your time to do. It is a long time; not in a moment. All the pilgrims were at the southern sphere of Atlantis, during which time the advance of the technological understanding had come to a great ebb. Already the northern parts of Atlantis were beginning to crumble and to fall under for they were misusing their light, you see. They could travel on the light. Their aeroships traveled on the light. They could not go around, for the light was not round in form; it followed a straight line. They wanted to go up. And they put their aeroships on the light and they went up, and they broke the stratum when they did so. And when they broke the stratum in the northern sphere, there came the great waters. And when the waters came, there was a great crumbling. A great pressure was emitted upon Terra. And the northern part that sits off your eastern coastline here began to fall and to crack and ebb as great mountains broke up and fell under the gust of waves. That is what it appeared to do. Not to be forewarned, they continued, although their land mass was falling into water, to go straight up.

There is a saying in your Book of Books that is written that was most appropriate for that time. And the saying says, "Behold in their last days they thrust themselves as eagles to plant their nests amongst the stars, and I brought them down." That was for them. That is not the future; that is the past.

And when they kept doing so, they kept breaking the stratum more. And behold that which was under the earth began to surface itself where the breaking of the stratum appeared. And all of the water that remained in the other stratum that is under what you now call your equator, that enveloped the bottom of Terra, became rigid. For no longer was there a consistency even in the water to carry the light evenly, to have warmth emitted. It was now displaced.

One by one this continent broke up and went under. I came to Atlantis in the last hundred years. And in the last hundred years, in what you call your Carolinas, the continent had broken up under them. They are remnants of mountain tops, all the way down.

The civilization of the *Atlanteans* at that particular point had degenerated itself into tyrants, tyrants who no longer knew how to use the technological advances that their forefathers had used, but of power through thought. The tyrants formed democracies. In the democracies the tyrants governed people through irrefutable law, not a republic. In a democracy of irrefutable law we — the Lemurians, the slums, the pilgrims, the dogs, the no things, the soulless, mindless waste of intellect — were being put to it. And that was my time. We did not have the great lights any longer. The great lights had been brought under when the last great quaking of Atlantis had occurred in the center of its metropolis of science. And all was destroyed from there.

There is a place that is called the Dead Horse Drones. It lies in your sea off your Eastern coast. Do you know there is no wind there? There have been mariners that have sailed into that awful, devilish place and the wind is no more and they perish there. It is there because there is no wind there. It is there where the scientific center of Atlantis thus rests. And from that there is also a great door. It is controlled by a great column of vacuum that leads into the inner civilization within your earth. Why is it dead there? You see, the attitude that was gathered up in the latter part of those days, the mediocrity of supreme intelligence in those latter days, emits still an attitude of sovereignty over all things. That is why there is no life there.

Now in the day of the Ram, when I was a little boy, it was not governed any longer by light but by tyrants, irrefutable law. And human life was nothing. Your red men, your Indians, why were they slaughtered? For once they were the ones that slaughtered the white peoples. For they were once the grand sovereigns of the entirety of Terra. And for them their karma has come full circle.

And in the land that they called the waste, they would put all things vile and dung heaps of the dead into this maze that connected the two continents of swamp and no land. Have you ever tried to fix a growing thing in a land that is always wet? That is where your rice came from, and the science of raising it came from your yellow peoples, for that was their homeland due to the *Atlanteans.*

In my time all I had to deal with were tyrants. Is that not enough? Is that more powerful than the light? Indeed it is. And in my time, beloved entity, they were direful times, for life was a no thing. It was nothing for one to pass a starving woman on the road. And all put kerchiefs of fine linen that were delved into jasmine and rose water upon their noses, you see, as they walked by us. We were stinking and wretched things. And that is when I was born.

How could I fight a light so great? I fought an attitude. And I ascended, beloved master, before the last cataclysm of Onai, before the last waters were dispensed from the stratum. I had the grand privilege of traveling through the Sudan and into Egypt and across the Persian lands — you would not even recognize them anymore — up into Indus, to the farthest northeastern corner of Indus to where the sun is especially wonderful.

And do you know why it sets east and west rather than north and south? What a pity for the sun to have set in the South, where it could no longer be seen, for the slim parts of the stratum still covered it. It was wonderful that it was caught up in the East and West kingdoms.

I had a wonderful delight of loving the sun and the moon and the wind and the stars and life fully in all of my life in the latter part of my years. And what we put under, entity, were tyrants, but to the grave misfortune only to be born again into religious tyrants which seemingly are deadlier. Are you enlightened?

When I was a little boy, indeed very small, the illusions of my times were very destitute. You have created in this your time flow a paradise because previous lives have taught you emotionally to create a more conducive consciousness in which you can expand. And when I was a little boy, life and its illusions were very arduous indeed, for my lineage was the dung of the earth. It was a waste of the earth. And our conscious view of more prominent races, my people and their lineage, would have been better off to go down with the whole lot of the seas that slaughtered the animals that lived on top of my land.

Contemplate for a moment being termed worthless, soulless, no-use-of, disgusting, revolting, vile, that you would tolerate being spat on, urinated on, dung on you and not allowed to wash it away, only with your tears. Contemplate you motherless, fatherless. Indeed contemplate you the dog in the street to have a greater nourishment than you who salivate and hunger for only something to kill the agony in your belly. Contemplate you what sort of a dream be I in. The beginning of the creation of man and his advent into his arrogant stupidity of intelligence, when so superb became he that the color of his skin or the cartouche upon his door was nothing, for there was nothing to eat for his arrogance, that was my dream.

Who chose to be Ramtha? I. Who has chosen to be you? You, like I, before entering into coagulated thought to what flesh is, chose the genetic patterns to which you would evolve from in your processes of understanding matter.

When you're at a greater level and you have never descended into the lower frequencies, you cannot understand. In the innocence of your being you have no knowledge to understand. Thus you do not understand the whole of God's kingdom; you are simply there.

I chose to be Ramtha. You chose to be you, your parents, the color of your skin, your gender, determined by your soul, and where you live, what you would call a geographical area; correct? So you are you.

In my life I was Ramtha. But into what Ramtha could be conceived, I was only the image of my greaters and never seen by my lessers. And the image of the greaters bestowed upon me disdainment: unliked, unloved, worthless vile of the earth. Thus that was my image to see what be I. And yet the lineage and the line, genetically speaking, that I had chosen to come forth in were grand in their knowingness of unseen values. And they held onto them, even onto their motherland, which now sits beneath the great sea. And those pilgrims held onto a knowingness that my superiors would not believe unless it was put into a reality, what you would call machines, kingdoms, power, order.

My lineage I chose because I issued forth from the house called Ramuste; Ram. In that house, the house is designated from soul emotion collectively. And the house from which I issued forth, its emotional understanding was the power to master. There were those that were issued from houses of emotional creativity. They created the machines, order, tyranny, segregation, hatred. But they were in the order to create progress.

When you issue from a house, it is clear for you to know which one. All you have to do is turn your eyes inward to find out where your honor lies and to what allegiance it is. I don't need to tell you; you already know.

And from this I chose to issue forth from Lemurians, Mu, against progress. I did not blame my mother that I had no father, nor did I blame my brother that our fathers were not of the same kin, nor did I blame my mother for our absolute poverty. I did not blame my God for what I had chosen openly to be. That is very much needed for you to learn, entities.

But what occurred from a house of emotion to master versus a house of progress was what it led up to; it became combat. Combat, know you what the term is? You don't have to be in a great army to know combat. All you have to know is a sharp tongue.

In my life as a little boy I watched my mother taken into the streets and have her sweetness taken from her. I watched in my life where we lived and the despise that was around me. And I watched when my mother was taken. I watched the child grow inside of her belly and knew who it was. I watched my mother weep. Why? That was very obvious. Would there be another sibling in the street to suffer as she had suffered in this promised land? I watched my mother bring forth a little sistern to life. I helped my mother because she was too weak to bear the child herself. And the little girl came forth yelling into the world. She wasn't happy. It was very obvious.

I scrounged in the streets and slayed dogs and wild fowl and stole the grain from the proprietors late in the evening, for I was very adept on my feet. And I fed my mother, who in turn suckled my little sister.

I did not blame my little sister for the death that would soon follow of my beloved mother, for the little girl suckled from my mother. All of her strength was given to the new life, that new life could continue forth. And my mother perished with the babe at her breast. There was nothing. There was no more.

And the little girl became diarrhetic. She could not hold what was coming into her body and passed it quickly from her body and lost all of the life in her body. And so they were gone.

And as a little boy I gathered up timbers and I laid them together. And I laid the timbers on top of my motheren and then stole away in the night and gathered fire. And I brought it and cuddled it and said a great prayer to my motheren and my little sistern and I loved them greatly. And I lit the timbers, for if I did not do so swiftly, the stench from them would cause agitation in the area and they would fling them into the desert and the hyenas would prey upon them and tear them apart. That they were not bothered, I set them to fire and burned them.

My hate for the red peoples, called the *Atlanteans*, was increased in my being like a great viper only as a little boy. And there was nothing left, for my brother was taken into subserviency into another city at the prey of a man and his needs for loin gratification.

My lineage worshipped and loved that which was beyond the stars, beyond your moon. They loved that which could not be identified. It was called the Unknown God. As a little boy I did not blame the Unknown God for his inability to love myself and my peoples and my motheren and my little sistern. I did not blame him; I hated him.

And in my times, no one died nobly of my peoples. There was no such thing as nobleness, virtue, indeed. So I found a great mountain that loomed in the distance, a very mysterious place. For if I climbed there I would get in touch with the Unknown God out here and proclaim my hatred for him and protest his unfairness. So I began my journey.

Now for that which is termed the rest of the story, there are a lot of you who know it well. But what drove me to conquer and to master, which was part of my soul emotion, was the desire to make it even. I created war, indeed, for there were no warring factions against the arrogance of the *Atlanteans*; none. I created it. I came from the great mountain, intimidated by the Unknown God and given a sword and told then to conquer myself. I could not turn the blade around and hack my head off; it was too long. My arms would not reach to that which is called the *stiffling* of the sword. But I wept a great deal. I got honor in my sword. And when I returned, I laid siege to Onai.

Now in my hostility and my desire to be noble and honorable to what I felt, I became a great entity. Know you what a hero is? Well, indeed I was one. And the hero salvages life and puts an undoing to wrongs of life without realizing I was also creating a wrong. But I was driven for ten years thereafter to slay tyranny and to make the color of my skin more appealing.

It was not until I was run through with such a great sword that I was to understand my purpose and why I was penetrated and had allowed it to occur. And from the tenth year of my march until sixty-three years, in your counting, it took me to gain enlightenment. But I am Ramtha. I desired it. I wanted it. I loved the Unknown God, whatever it was. And in sixty-three years of contemplating and understanding where the hate came from, who created it and why, come I to terms with myself. And when I did, my mind became free like a bird, to soar in the heavens of thought, wisdom, creation, understanding.

I hated, and I had the desire to master it. The primitive way was to slay it in others, to slay the reflection of what I despised in others and do away with it and to give everything to the poor, wretched creatures who didn't even possess a soul. Well, even after all of that I could not sleep and slumber in your evenings, for I was a tormented entity. For though I had all things, I had not peace, which is the result of a tender understanding of self, I, Ramtha.

To gain knowingness, you have to humble yourself and look at who you are — not what your mirror tells you, but who you are — and see what is within you, the individual sublime God. And you have to cease to holding self as prisoner. The lot of you do it, save one entity in this room, one entity. Know you what a prison is? I can manifest you a dungeon or two so that you can understand what truth feels like when it is behind bars and the rats are eating at your feet and the lice are crawling in your hair and the worms are coming from the stench in your dung.

You're a prisoner of yourself, as I was. For though the desire to master, which come I from, was there, I did not know and understand flesh, coagulated thought and its needs, desires and its consciousness on a lower plane of existence. I did not know what it would take. So I ended up in a great conflict, at a great and terrible time in your time, all past, in which things had to be righted in consciousness and within self.

You entities, know you how you imprison your truth? You don't know who you are. I was a filthy Lemurian, soulless. Do you know who you are? Do you know the virtue that lies within you? Do you know what you have come here to do? All of your blames for your life you have put and cast at the feet of others, the lot of you have. Everyone is responsible for your unhappiness. That is a great blunder but also a great learning.

When you know who you are — in my life that took sixty-three years to learn that — you will look at yourself to see readily who has created all the destinies that you have lived by self-choice. And all of the unhappiness is by self-choice. And all of the happiness is by self-choice. But it was you and no one else.

When you can humble yourself to look at you, look at you, feel you, and ask yourself why and then say, "I know why," and become reasonable with self, then you have taken away the bars from truth, which is the bird that soars in heaven called happiness, virtue, oneness, and peace. I slumbered in the latter part of my sixty-three years of enlightenment.

I slumbered because I was a peaceful man. I had come to terms with all things. I had made peace with all things and learned to love and to respect and admire my greatest adversaries, for I was their threat. I learned to love them because I learned to love the elegance called Ramtha, indeed.

Your life is life after life after life. One million years can be lived in one lifetime. Know why it takes you so long and so many lives? Because of the inability to look at who you are. You judge another and indeed that judgment you have put forth will one day decide to live for your better good, to understand others better through the means called self. But for the most part, in all of your lives you have learned but one thing in those lives. You have been slow to accelerate knowingness because you have refused to look at who has created it; refused to. Well, I can tell you, entities, that the lot of you have lived every conceivable entity that has ever been created in the genetic loin and womb of woman and man, and every color. And you have been the least, like a Lemurian, to the most arrogant, like an *Atlantean*. You have been all of them, all of them. But why not in one life accelerate what can take a moment to proclaim and in the compassion within the soul to reveal self, therefore looking at who you are.

And I began to understand who was Ramtha. I jolly well loved what I was, indeed. And I felt very pleased at the entity, so became I. Why? Because I was at peace with the Unknown God who I had found through me, me. And I loved the unique, powerful, and wonderful way I created my destiny and led my people into greater understanding. And all I had done before did not matter when I forgave myself and understood why, for it no longer tormented me. It no longer hurt. It no longer drove me into conquering.

I have taught you very well. But I say to you — and the lot of you still do not know what I am saying — that all that you have been you have been for the purpose of gaining understanding, love. Man's creation of right and wrong, of judgmental truth, also created fear and guilt and the inability to progress in a spiritual life. When I speak of spiritual, I speak of all life, not just that which is something wonderful to speak of in philosophic ways on certain days of your week, but all days. And then you become inhibited and drown in your own sorrow and lost in your own scorn and denied by your own self. I tell you, entities, all that you have done in all of your lives, it is all right. God the Source, that is the very vibrance of this wondrous molecular structure, has not judged you; it does not know judgment. It does not know perfection, a complete limitation. It only is. It is the Isness that loves, that is all itself. And that self is the encompassing power of all of you that are here, all peoples everywhere.

God never judged you, never hailed you to be a saint or a demon. You only did that to yourself again, not knowing who you are. If the Father who in all that He is has found jolly goodness in your wondrous being, then you have gained. And you still have life this next moment to live, to exuberate divine self. I assure you, beloved entities, when I tell you you are God, live it so you can see and understand why you have been the way you have been, indeed.

So the Unknown God was all things: twilight, the night bird and its rustle in the bush, the wild fowl in their seasonal morning flights, the laughter of children and the magic of lovers, the ruby of wine and the sweetness of honey. It is all things, all things that are perpetual.

I knew the Unknown God in these understandings. There was no teacher to teach me this. The Ram, the master, the conqueror, was in me to understand. It was my need to understand. So I was left with my great wound to heal, to sit, to ponder, and to think. All I had was myself, indeed, alone, sitting on a great rock — not in something as wondrous as this. In that I reasoned forgiveness before there was such a word. And I reasoned self before there was such an identity. And I reasoned God and self as one, to solve the mystery.

What I did in my life I have taught you eloquently and manifested boldly for you in your life, that you would have the opportunities to exhibit that same desire to humble yourself to see who you are. And for the lot of you who still close your eyes, I cannot teach the only impossibility there ever was: a closed mind. They do not hear nor do they perceive, for it endangers their cloistered truth of security. You, how know you yourself? Like the dove that is in the prison, forgive you. The Father has always forgiven you. It has understood.

Look at what you are. Look at it. Look at your anger; why are you angry? Look at your jealousy; why are you jealous? Look at your envy; why are you envious? Look at your insecurities and understand why. Look at your judgments; why do you judge? Look at your unmercy; why aren't you merciful? And look at your laughter; where is it?

You contemplate this that I have told you. You do not have the patience to endure for sixty-three years, for you are very rapid. Impatience is scornful. You need it completely now. But in my life, that was my life. And that made me who be I this hour unto you and has preserved the personality self called Ramtha the Great, that the infinite knowingness of God could come forth from this established vessel to teach you in familiar tones.

If you want to be as I am, think like I think, then make it applicable to however way and ceremony that you do, but do it.

# II.

# Consciousness and Energy

reetings my beautiful entities and beginners. I salute you. Let's
have a drink. You're going to need it. The water represents that
which is termed the Source, consciousness everlasting. It is, as
it were, an appropriate medium to salute that which is termed God within
us all. Now let us begin the session by saluting our divinity rather than our
fragility.

O my beloved God,
Somewhere within me
Come forth this day
And open my mind,
Open my life,
That that which I hear
I may experience.
O my beloved God, of this day
Bless my beingness and that which I learn.
So be it.
To life.

I am Ramtha the Enlightened One. I am the entity who spoke all those words that you've read about, that indeed you've listened to, that touched you. It was, as it were, a ringing of truth. Don't be dismayed about the body I am in. Be dismayed at the body you're in.

I unfolded in this consciousness nigh a long time ago in your time and of that which is termed in this body. This is that which is termed an arrangement, as you would call it, prior to the incarnation of this being (JZ Knight, the channel). You're here to learn that God doesn't look like anybody but everyone and everything. Moreover, you're here to learn that God in Its most exalted quality can be viewed in something as simple as a tree or you.

I did not come here, unfold here, for the purpose of creating a body that was awe-inspiring, delicious and beautiful, because that has been the idol of worshippers for eons, even today. Beauty has taken that which is termed physical characteristics. It is no longer spiritual, the inert. And you worship it. But it makes you small because it's a fleeting quality; it is. And it blooms only *smally* in one's physical life and then it fades.

I came, as it were, outrageous, as an enlightened being. And what mean that, an enlightened being? What is your term for enlightenment? It means one who is aware, who has far vision. An enlightened being is one who is pure consciousness manifested in Spirit or mind. And that means that an enlightened being will have a greater quality of the richness of its Spirit than it will in its body. An enlightened entity is one who does not see itself as its body but as that aspect that is unified with all life. That's an enlightened entity. One who is not is one who views itself separate, special, different from all other life forms. They are the entities that are ignorant.

So I am an enlightened being because in my life and in the times that I knew, I had a grand and wondrous opportunity to be my man-self, to be a human being, to create war, to do away with tyrants. What a lofty goal, eh? But it was not until I betrayed myself that I became humbled off of my arrogance. And in that humbleness when I held onto my life by, as you would call it, a gossamer thread, I wondered what was the purpose of my life and poor, wretched people. And it wasn't until every day that I was grasping for life, and every day I made a mark that that day I lived through, that I realized that life in and of itself was the prize.

I'm called enlightened because what I learned transcended my physical self. The warrior died; the conqueror passed away. The arrogance, like smoke from a late fire, danced into the night air and disappeared. My ignorance disappeared.

So I became a spiritual entity. And what does that mean? It means that I used my brain and my body and my emotional body not for the sake of conquering, achieving goals, and laying waste and resurrection of the earth. I changed. Instead of becoming the solitude, man-to-man, force-to-force, I gathered myself up day after day, little by little, to become a personality that found value not in conquest of this realm but found value in the conquest of ignorance.

So then how did I become enlightened? Because by being a piece of the Unknown God I made up my mind that I wanted to be exactly that. And so God, because God loves — and we understand that in that it gives, never takes, only gives — God within gave me exactly what I wanted to be: that which is all things, that which can share love with all life.

And so what did I become? I did not become a better man. I became a spiritual being, a God; not a man. And that was what I wanted to be. If the Unknown God was faceless, then It was the power and urges in nature itself. That is what I wanted to be because that most defined God to me not people, not being a man, but being a being acting upon the knowingness that it is a part of all life. That's what I became.

So why was I called enlightened? I was enlightened because I became my Spirit rather than my body. Today I am here in this time, as you know it, in another body. You have come to hear me because you have read my words, you have heard them, you have listened to other people, you have seen a wonderment in their life. Now you come as men, women, and children, a Spirit small contained within the body. The job of your Spirit has been to keep you alive. That's the only reason you've ever used it. And the only reason you didn't die sooner than coming here is because you used your Spirit to keep you alive, and you've never abused it so much that it has abandoned your body yet. That's all you've used it for. But it's why you're here.

Because inasmuch as it cannot be seen, but rather felt, is that which I am. You came here to see me as the Spirit, as you're getting to do right now. I appear to be that which is termed ordinary, naturally. The teaching then is that God lives in you as what you have defined as a Spirit. But it's just kept you alive. And if you were to see that Spirit, you would never see it as looking like your body. Well, I am here in a body that seems contradictory to my terms: It is female and I am male. But it is most wonderful because it is to teach men and women that God is both and neither. I need to teach you that what you've been thinking around in that brain of yours is not necessarily all there is but also to teach you that what you are, you cannot see.

So most appropriately I came here to talk to people that I once knew in a time that seems far remote from this time, and yet that time and this time are happening at the same moment. I'm here to teach you what I never taught you, because I abandoned you for my greater reality. Now I am not teaching you to follow me; you can't. Even when you die you cannot because, when you die, you're only going to get the gift of life that's equal to your ability to accept. And the only thing that you've ever accepted has been your life, no matter how it is. That's what is important to you. Hunger is important to you, pain is important to you, being disoriented because you don't like reality, that's important to you. It is important to you to be a woman; it's important to you to be a man. You see, all of these are physical in nature and can obliterate the Spirit. You can lose your focus on God quicker in the midst of hunger than anything else.

I came to teach you what I knew and what I learned. I came to teach you that even if you die, you are not going to be enlightened. You'll be a spiritual being but your mind won't be there.

There isn't one God; all is God. This isn't the only life you've ever lived. These bodies, they are like garments. You're just wearing this body as this garment in this time flow. You've worn many of them. So you say, "Why can't I remember?" You can't remember because you're not enlightened. You understand? In your last life, you didn't get any further than you've gotten in this one. If the only thing you're concerned about was that last life, then the only aspect that you used was the brain for your personality then. That lifetime was just about the body, as it always is. So when that body died, along with that brain, you can't remember because the body and that brain are gone. All you can remember is this life and you can't remember most of the days in your life because you haven't lived them. You were absent from them.

Oh, you have lived eons. You are in evolution. God gave you eternal life. What does that mean? That means when you die — this afternoon, tomorrow morning — that your body is going to perish but you're going to rise in your spiritual body. But the spiritual body again is only as great as the mind that occupies it, which is what you're cultivating now. That's eternal life.

You'll be reborn and you won't remember today. You know why you won't remember today? Because your brain in the future was not here today but your Spirit was.

So what I came to teach you is not to follow me because that's impossible, and I don't want to be worshipped. I want you to worship you. The greatest temple of God that was ever built was never made out of stone and gold and silver and jewels. The greatest temple of God happens to be the human body, and that body is where the Spirit occupies itself in this realm; that's the temple.

Now if what you learn lifts you inside, then the lifting inside is the feeling of the Spirit. If you come here and you're tired or you're hungry or bored, that is your body's mind, not your Spirit.

If you are lifted by what you're going to learn, now we are talking to that which cannot be seen inside of you but that which you are inside of you. It's going to make an enormous amount of sense. What is going to be the only objection of today and tomorrow? Your monkey-mind, your human brain. You know why? Because if I asked you to explain to your neighbor how broad is the level of your acceptance — how broad, how deep, how high is the level of your acceptance — that is what belief is. You can never ever manifest in your life that which you do not accept. You only manifest that which you accept. So how broad is your acceptance? Is it greater than your doubt? What are the limitations of your acceptance? Is that why you're sick? Is that why you're old? Is that why you're unhappy? Because the level of your acceptance is unhappiness. That's all you get, you know. You don't get anything greater than that because anything greater than that lies in the Spirit. So your Spirit is making you unhappy because you're telling it to.

So the only teaching you're going to have problems with today is the level of acceptance in your carnal mind; that's this up here (the brain). If you're the sort of person that is a victim to your own guilt, if you've done a lot of wretched and awful things and think you're so very special because you're so guilty, then you're going to have difficulty with what I tell you because I am telling you that you create your reality. And if you're a victim, it is because you made it that way. And you're not going to like that because you want someone else to be responsible for your pain, your limitation, and your lack. And I'm going to tell you it's your responsibility and you're not going to like that. The Spirit agrees, but the brain doesn't buy that because it can say who hurt it, it can say who disappointed it, it can say why it doubts. It's someone else's fault, never oneself. The arrogance of the human brain, eh?

Also you're going to have difficulty with the concept that you're all God, because there are some of you that still like to believe that God is a piece of real estate called heaven and that He — rather She — is pulling all the strings. That's why if something goes rotten in your life, you can say it's God's will. "God has a gripe about me."

God is a convenient image in heaven because as long as God sits there, He's the one that will punish you for your iniquities, you know: your lack, your lack of love, of caring; when you think bad thoughts you're going to get punished by God somewhere in heaven. And when you want to be saved, you want somebody to be able to save you. You know why? Because you don't believe you can save yourself.

God actually works a wonderful part in religion. But I tell you that the only piece of real estate called heaven is that which is within you and what you allow yourself to believe. Then your God can start right away today forgiving you of your guilt, forgiving you of your lack. Today you can stop being a victim. Today you can stop being sick. Today you can stop believing in the devil and you can start believing in yourself. Some of you will not like it because you need to have a savior. You're not going to like it because you need to have a moment when God's going to return and get you.

This will be *contraire* to what you believe, because I say to you and what I'm going to teach you is about yourself and what lies inside you. There are most of you here that don't believe you can manifest anything. You have accepted your lack. This will be *contraire* to you. But for many of you, the axiom of "believe in yourself and everything is possible" will be accepted.

But wait a minute. What is the problem here? Well, I think we found it. It's called believing in yourself. That is what this school is about, fighting and conquering a self that is only indigenous to this life and being greater than our greatest appetites. We are learning to accept what our human brain doesn't and teaching it to.

This school is about resurrecting the Spirit in you, the God in you, to do the miraculous. I am not here to be a savior; I never said I was. I don't want to be. I am here to teach you what I know, which is a lot. I have the patience of the eons to make that happen. I desire you do as well.

What you're going to learn is to glorify God in you. And it's going to be a lot of work. But in the end you're still going to have your body, but your level of acceptance is going to be unlimited indeed. You know why? Because you're going to do miraculous things that will cause you to believe further in yourself.

That is not to say that it is the Golden Way; it's a treacherous way. Every step along the way your *altered* ego, which is the personality of this body, is always there to assassinate you. When you become an enlightened entity, it will be because you have conquered your *altered* ego. I would say to you then you who are not clinging to that gossamer thread of life, what have you got to lose? A day here, a day there, an hour in focus? What have you got to lose? You know what you've got to lose? Only your doubt. What do you have to lose in accepting the miraculous rather than denying it? What have you got to lose? I tell you, beginners, what you will lose in this life are the limitations of this life as you have once known them to be and you will gain an eternal life.

Eternal Life? Did I not say that everyone will awaken from the death bed? Indeed I did. But what will be different about you? Because you are going to learn to visit the kingdom of heaven and that dimensional realm while you're alive in this body, thereby expanding your realm of acceptance. And if you pass, and you choose to pass, you're not going to go where everyone else goes. Perhaps you will never have to come back here again. Perhaps you are so lofty that another galaxy with another race of beings that are superbrilliant will be your next parents because you are ready to know what is unfathomable here to know.

Now everyone who comes to this school is always tested. But do you know who tests them? Themselves. Spirit left alone is fragile and is always given an opportunity for it to develop on its own. But if the person's mind, their *altered* ego, becomes greater and gets a stronghold into daily life, it will diminish the Spirit that is very small and fragile. And what happens? Then soon they return to doubting and lacking and disbelieving. And they start looking for everything outside of them to sort of give them comfort and nourishment because they have lost the power inside of them.

Then they come back to school. Imagine having a stampede come back to this august body, a stampede of wild Spirits and hesitant *altered* egos. Imagine all the cleanup work that has to go on for the first few days. And what is the cleanup work? Even my greatest students in this august body have to be cleaned up. What does that mean? They have to be told again that they are greater than their body and that what exists in the kingdom of God is greater than their doubt. They have to be reminded of their divinity and they have to be pushed into their disciplines and retaught the power to manifest. "Oh, yes, oh, yes, now I remember." Imagine if I only have a week with them. We are talking four days of cleanup work, three days of just getting to another level and learning to accept something that they didn't accept before, three days of accomplishment, and then they leave.

Do I have students who have changed since they came and sat in your seats? Oh, yes. Do I have students that can do miraculous things? Yes, I do. Do I have students that can't do miraculous things? Yes, I do. Why is there a difference? Why can some and some not?

Do you know the answer?

Now lesson number one: "You get exactly what you want." Will you write that down.

Next sentence I want you to write down is, "Consciousness and Energy create reality."

And the next sentence I want you to write down is, "Consciousness and Energy and a brain create mind."

Do you know what consciousness means? What if we say something simple like "Consciousness, it is the fabric of life." That's what it is. I didn't say it was the mind of life; I said it was the fabric of life. And because consciousness is an awareness, then consciousness must already contain energy. So Consciousness and Energy are inextricably combined. They are one and the same. There is no such thing as unconscious energy. Are you still with me?

Now Consciousness and Energy creating the nature of reality would be very simple to explain to your partner. It simply means that reality could not exist without Consciousness and Energy because reality is, after all, self-aware.

Now the brain. Put your hands up on this sort of melon that you have up on your shoulders. It houses the greatest organ ever created. You got it in there. Large, eh? It's nice; it holds your face up very nice. The brain is different than consciousness, although consciousness is what gives cells their life. The brain does not create consciousness; it creates thought. Will you write that down. The brain creates thought; that's its job.

Now one thought equals mind. Will you put that down. Mind is equated by one thought.

Listen to me. You get confused, and why shouldn't you? All of these scholars running around tossing about the words consciousness and mind and the brain and no one knows how they actually work. But I'll tell you how they work. Even though they are only words, they do have a definition. Consciousness and Energy are the Source. When it gives life, it gives life as a thought. The body, the human body, contains a brain, and that brain is the vehicle for streams of Consciousness and Energy. It's its power source.

The brain's job is to take impulses of Consciousness and Energy at the neurological level and create thoughts. The brain actually chops up the stream of consciousness into coherent thought forms that are lodged in the neurosynaptic pathways in the brain.

Now the brain can remember a thought; that's its job. So your brain is there to function with the stream of Consciousness and Energy moving through it, firing the synaptic points, giving you images up here (in the brain). Mind is not Consciousness and Energy; it's the product. Mind is the product of consciousness on the brain creating thought forms or memory. When we take all of those memories and put them together, then you can say, "I like the mind of that person."

Now, beginners, is there a difference between the terms Consciousness and Energy and mind? (Yes.)

Now before we go any further, I want you to understand something. You're learning a philosophy here, not a truth. None of this is the truth. You're learning a philosophy. And what does that mean? It's a teaching. The teaching is about a theoretical concept called reality that we have said so far has everything to do with you. But it's not the truth. Truth is relative. Only what you know is truth. If you don't know anything else, it's not the truth.

If someone tells you that there is a twenty-third universe besides this one, they may be telling you from scientific observation; it's their truth. But is it yours? It's not your truth. It's a philosophy, like most things in your life.

Why is it not the truth? Because you haven't experienced the twenty-third universe, and only until you have experienced the twenty-third universe is it a truth.

Now don't be afraid, I beseech you, to learn what I am about to teach you because it does marvelous things. Accept it as a philosophy and that the truth will emerge from the philosophy once you apply it. So now you're safe. We're not converting anyone.

Everyone in antiquity always endeavored to teach what is not seen in symbols. So they always said that God was like the sunshine or the light of Ra and that that was Consciousness and Energy. Thus when we saw the light — you've heard that term, haven't you? — when we saw the light then we were what? Enlightened.

Now Consciousness and Energy in symbolism are like the sun because in its winds it radiates a stream of consciousness, that that stream of consciousness is picked up by the human brain and put forward into thought forms, which they in turn plant something or see something or create something.

Now this idea of the light — you know, "Go to the light" — that is an archetype in human consciousness, simply because the only way for the human brain to decipher the reality of God and Consciousness and Energy is to see it as light lighting up the darkness. We understand that in a dark room we can't see anything. But the moment a shaft of light comes into the room or a little flame is lit then suddenly the light itself, coming at right angles on solid objects, gives a refraction of depth and we begin to see. So the idea of enlightenment came from the concept that ignorance is done away with a light of truth, and they call it consciousness.

Now it is not really a light. It's only seen as a light and described as one. When we say then that if God is this form here, radiating this stream of light to all entities, then that radiating light is God itself being felt in these entities. That is how it's been described.

The brain must have a stream of consciousness in order to be called alive. When probes are hooked up to the brain to see if there is anyone home, what is revealed is the brain's ability to process Consciousness and Energy by the firing of that which is termed the neurons in the brain. These neurons fire at different frequencies, and science has learned to determine if anyone's at home by the electrical firing in the brain. If there is a reading, it is assumed that this person is alive. But why aren't they awake? Well, because they're in a coma. But they're alive, yes.

Isn't that a remarkable, astounding understanding for you. They're unconscious but they're alive. What's keeping them alive? The Spirit of Consciousness and Energy. Why aren't they awake? Because they're not processing thought on a conscious level. When you're conscious and aware, your eyes open and you start processing thought. What is processing thought? In the neurology of the brain, different parts of it begin to fabricate holographic thought forms and then analyze those forms. Now we have a person who is awake and aware. And maybe they only have their eyes closed but they're awake and they're aware; they're present. They are interacting with their environment through the mechanics of thought.

The person's ability to think gives them a mind. So how great is your mind?

Have you learned everything there is to learn in this lifetime? Do you know it all, absolutely all of it?

Now if Consciousness and Energy are streaming towards you and through you every day, then what keeps you from knowing all that there is? Your mind; you only know what you know.

Now when we talk about "you" then, we start to separate you from the whole and talk about you as an individual. What makes you an individual? The way you look, the way you talk, the way you think. Well, all of those are the results of the way you think. And your mind is the sum total of all of the philosophy that you learned in school. You say, "I graduated from school." What does that mean? "That means that I remembered everything they taught me and I passed all the tests based on my memory." But did you experience it? "No."

So then your brain is full of theoretical philosophy that you've agreed must be the truth, but it isn't. The person who taught you this, it's not even their truth. It's the truth of the individual who did the discovery.

Now what is in your head? Everything that is in your head is everything your parents taught you, everything that your schools taught you, everything your history taught you, everything your culture taught you. But how much of it is the truth? In other words, is anyone home or is this just a recording?

You know why no one creates miracles any longer except in the field of technology? Because everyone has assumed that everything that they have learned in their head is the truth. Miracles only come at the expense of expectancy. Does that make sense to you? In other words, it's what you didn't learn, it's what you don't know as truth, that you expect it to happen and it does; that's truth.

So your mind is filled with so much gibberish. And how much superstition do you have inside of you? Do you walk under ladders? Do you believe white is good and black is bad? Shame on you. Do you feel guilty? Shame on you. Do you still feel guilty? Shame on you.

Now here's the point. The point is that one of the reasons that you're so bored with life is because you can only do what you know as the truth. You know, that happens every Saturday night, that happens every Sunday morning, that happens at work. You're bored with your job and you're bored with your life. Do you know why? Because you keep doing the only thing you know how to do and that's the only truth that you have. Everything else is conjecture. So how great is your mind? It's only as great as your truth.

Now what's the purpose then? Imagine what your Spirit is thinking. Have you ever imagined your Spirit on Saturday night? "Give it up. Are we doing this again today?" Imagine your Spirit, you know, your God. "What is wrong with you? Can't you do anything else? Can't you think on your own? Can't you shut up long enough to let me talk to you? You have bad breath." Imagine when your Spirit's talking to you. "I don't want to go to work today. I don't want to do the same old thing today. Do you know why I don't want it? Because it's me that you use to do the same old thing every day. And I'm getting smaller and smaller and smaller. And if you're starting to look like a prune, it's because you've used me up."

Imagine your Spirit when you're going to be spiteful to someone, because it empowers you to be spiteful to someone. I know what this feels like. Imagine your Spirit looking back in horror as your monkey-mind proceeds to attack viciously. And like a puppet it's being used to slug it out with some innocent person. Imagine your Spirit sitting there shouting, "Will you shut up. Why must you be this way? We do not want to make war; we want to make love. Love this person." Imagine that voice in your head at the moment of your greatest tempest. And you're angry and it says to you, "Calm down. Let's love. This is us that we are attacking." Imagine that voice. You don't want to hear that voice. You tell it to shut up and you get even madder and you punch even wilder. Imagine your Spirit; what else is it supposed to do?

You know, the reason you're growing old and you're getting an awful lot of diseases is that your Spirit has had it with you because you're supposed to grow. That's why you're here. What does growing mean? It doesn't mean that your body is to grow; it means that your wisdom is to grow. Your Spirit is the life force that you use up in one lifetime. It's large when you're a child; it's all over the place. And as you start spilling your seed and having your season of blood and as you start forming opinions about the world, it starts to get smaller and smaller and smaller because you're using your Spirit up to create with.

Now you know why you're dying? It's because you've used up a vital energy source of eternity in the forms of created thoughts. One of these days that Spirit is not going to wait to get rid of you. It's going to shake, shake, shake, shake, until you fall off. How could a Spirit get to be so ungodly? That's just the point; it is.

You're here to grow, my beloved people. You're here to create reality, not to continue status quo. You're here to grow in knowledge, philosophy, and then in truth. You're here to live, not be afraid of life. You're here to use your brain to create thoughts and to conquer ignorance.

What happens when a person becomes enlightened? They conquer their ignorance. What does that mean? It means that they developed their Spirit rather than their *altered* ego, their personality, and their body. And they work every day in embodiment of that energy. So what happens to them? They don't ever really grow old; rather they have dynamic energy. They can create. And their level of acceptance is extraordinary. If you ask them do you believe in this, they will always say yes; they will never say no. They will say, "I have experienced that already. I've owned that." What does that mean? "That means I created it as a philosophy; I manifested it as an experience; I experienced it and, boy, was I in trouble. But after the experience, I know about it. I have wisdom. I have truth."

Now that doesn't mean you have to be a goody-two-shoe or three-shoe, whatever you want. It doesn't mean that. New Age is not new age; it is forever age. What it means is being greater than your body and being greater than your prejudice, being greater than your lack. And that's not having a positive mental attitude. Because if a person has a positive mental attitude, it simply means that they really have a negative mental attitude in which they are trying desperately to have a positive mental attitude. So we have a veneer of positive possibility. I want you to change and to be it.

Consciousness and Energy create the nature of reality. That reality created the human body and with it its greatest organ, the human brain. The brain does not create Consciousness and Energy; it is the instrument of it, a machine. Its job is to take Consciousness and Energy and to freeze-frame it into memorized biochemical thought, that that thought then can be added onto to create reality, and that whatever sits focused in the brain as a thought is created in front of you in the time flow. The idea is to take Consciousness and Energy, the virgin, and create thought that is evolutionary to be greater and to think greater, so that in turn creates your life greater. Then God, the Spirit, is now evolving in you. And what is happening within you happens outside of you.

The discipline of Consciousness and Energy means this: That one of the first principles learned in school is how to still the mind and find the place called the Void. The Void is the Mother/Father Principle. It is where Consciousness and Energy spring from. And by moving energy from the base of your spine to the midbrain, between that which is termed your neocortices, that energy is given to the brain so that the brain is stilled and just idling, so that then who you are disappears, what you feel disappears, what you're worried about disappears. All other things are wiped clean in the brain. Because if the brain is the mechanism for creating tangible reality via thoughts, then we have to clean it up and get it pure, so that whatever we place here in the frontal lobe area of the brain as a focused conscious thought will manifest in absolute clarity.

# III.
## Origins in the Void

I salute the God within you. Pray let us never forget where God resides. And let's have a drink.

> O my beloved God,
> I call forth
> That which I learn
> This day.
> I expect
> To experience it.
> God Bless My Life.
> So be it.
> To Life.

Now mind creates reality. Every day of your life has been that which is termed a product of the way that you've thought. If we can understand this process and expand that which is termed your level of acceptance and indeed your level of understanding, you should, according to the philosophy, experience truth by manifesting it in your own life. So I want you to be able to speak today everything that I have taught you, to be able to draw it out, to be able to use your hands simple as a child, and to be able to express what I am teaching you, that you may be able to express it to someone else. Participate in everything that I ask you to do. If you do, you will be enriched.

You are little children. There are civilizations and entities on other planets in other galaxies in other dimensions in other time flows that are much more advanced than you are. However, having said that, there are other entities on a few other worlds that are a little behind you, but not much.

You are little children. You are, as it were, part of a community called God. And what we have referred to you for eons is a term that is most befitting to the human drama and that is the term "forgotten Gods." You forgot about your divinity and got wrapped up in your physicality, your material self.

# In the Beginning

Now let us go back to the beginning, you know, the beginning that happened only a moment ago. How did this all begin? The teaching that I am going to give you today may be filled with verbiage contradiction. However, there is a level of understanding that transcends words. So words become that which is termed a cripple's tool in order to explain that desire that cannot be expressed. We are going to be talking today about how all of this, the vastness of space and time, all came about and where did you come from, why are you here, and what are you doing not getting to where you should be going.

Now take out a piece of paper, clear, clean paper. Let it have no thing upon its surface. We are going to talk about an enigma in terms of two-dimensional expression. I want you to repeat this word: the Void. Again now, the Void. Let us determine what the definition of this word should be. The Void is vast. And yet in its vastness there is nothing. So it is one vast no thing. "No thing" means elemental, even thought; there is nothing, no thing. So it is a vast nothingness, nothing. And yet in the face of and in the space of nothingness exist potentials. Thus we would say that the Void, although it is a vast no thing, is potentially everything.

I want you to repeat this: "One vast nothing materially." Say it. "All things potentially."

One vast nothing materially, all things potentially; that is the Void. The Void, to that which is termed a finite mind, is difficult to conceive. So perhaps the most graduated visual that can be utilized is to think of space and all of the stars and planets and gas clouds and nebulae that are therein and see it as far as you can see. And then in the next moment, extinguish all of the light from space. Now we have a close mental concept of the Void, one vast nothing.

Now how old is one vast nothing? It's timeless because time is a potential that will spring from it.

So the Void has always been.

Now do you experience the Void in your normal life? Have you allowed your mind to rest or take a pause naturally, and you are staring with your eyes transfixed? And in the moment that you're staring and transfixed, you're not thinking of anything. Empty. That is the Void.

The Void in its alwaysness is called the Mother/Father Principle or it is called the Source, the Source in which all life springs from. But how does life spring from a no-concept? How does the Void give life to that which it is not?

So this is what happened: One morning at 10:30, Tuesday, I believe, the Void did a spectacular thing.

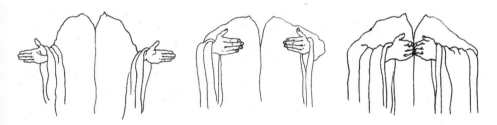

Void Contemplating Itself

The thing was that it contemplated itself; contemplated itself. Now I want you to spread your arms out like little children. Contemplation, as a visual, is seen in this way. Where the left and the right hands come together is the center of the magnet. Where the negative and the positive come together is the center of the magnet. The magnet's center is neither negative nor positive. It just is. The Void, being one vast nothing, contemplated itself. And the moment that it did, a moment was born.

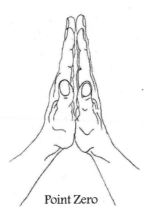

Point Zero

Now I want you to take your blank piece of paper and I want you to turn it in on itself. And where it meets I want you to take a writing instrument and put a little black mark there. That is to give you a picture of how all of this began.

Now remember this is simple, elementary. The Void contemplating itself created an echo of itself. In other words it created an alteredness of itself, and we recognize that in this dot. This is the first time a potential is born out of the Void that always was. This potential, where it contemplated itself, becomes the echo but concentrated. It is an evolution.

Now this is what you began as. This entity here is contained as Consciousness and Energy. In this was your beginning and yet you have not quite begun. You have only been contemplated upon by the Void. All of this is the Void, and we are seeing it in that which is termed two-dimensional linear time. But this spot here now becomes a reference point. This then is called "God." So I want you to write beside this "God I Am" straightaway.

This contemplation point is Consciousness and Energy beginning. This is the Mother/Father Principle that gave it life and this is where you started.

Now the Void talks to this little entity and it says, "Good afternoon. I have longed for your presence in my midst. I am delighted with your countenance. I want you to make of me whatever you want to do. I am no longer alone. You are now with me. Go and make of me whatever you please."

When your mother and father told you that, when you were little entities, you got into trouble. So you ran around the house and you ran around outside and you did all the things you wanted to do and then you came in and only found out that that wasn't exactly what they had in mind. How many of you remember that? The only difference is with this parent there was no constriction; there was a permission to grow and to expand.

So now imagine what you would think. "Go and make of me whatever you want to do." Understand there is no time in this Void. And if there is no time, there is no distance. And if there's no distance, there's no space.

So here's what you start thinking, "All right, I'll run over here. This looks fun." So the moment you run anyplace, you're back at the start because "here" is "there" in the Void. There is no time, so "over there" doesn't exist. The starting point is all points.

Then you get a little frustrated and you say, "Well, that is all right, then I'll go down here." But what is "down" to the Void? So you end up down here and you say, "Aha." But the moment you perceive that you're down, you're really back where you started because in the Void there is no time. So everywhere is the same.

This entity was all over the Void but never went anywhere. We can only anticipate from this point of reflection how many eons that entity must have stayed there trying to be all that its parent had said for it to be, because "all" was certainly up for a new understanding. Everywhere this consciousness threw itself, it already was. So it never went anywhere.

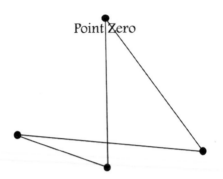

Point Zero

Then one day, Friday, as it was sitting there, it contemplated itself. Every time you contemplate yourself, you evolve. So it turned all of itself in on itself. And as soon as it did that, the point of contemplation was created. If you take both of your hands and hold them in prayer position with a slight separation, this represents that little point that turned in on itself.

The moment it turned in on itself, do you see how it became divided? How many of you see? And the moment it did, it was two instead of one.

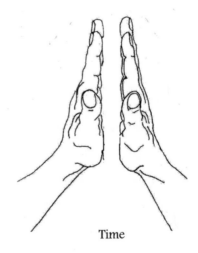

Time

Well, now Consciousness and Energy have company; it has someone else here. So the Void that gave birth to it, in turn gave birth to this. What is this? This is yet a lower aspect of the original point of contemplation.

Hold your hands up. This space here is very unique in the Void because for the first time we have two points of consciousness. And yet between those two points we also have a new reality, and that reality is called time.

Why is time existent only here? Because we have a distance between two points of reality. If we close these hands, is there any time? No. Agree? Wonderful. Well, now we have the second great creation: We have time, distance, and space that are offset by another consciousness. So how many of you have heard of the seventh level of heaven? This is the seventh level of heaven. This is where we began.

Now close them back up; now we're one. Separate them; we are two. How fast is the reality on the seventh level of heaven? (He closes and reopens his hands over and over.) Well, let me ask you: If you had the consciousness as a seventh-level entity and if you had a thought, how long would it take to manifest? (He closes his hands.) That's all.

Now we have creation right here. This (left hand) is the God and this (right hand) is the mirror consciousness. Now we have life happening. Between these two hands exists a whole reality just like this Earth plane, except it's the seventh plane.

And after you lived here for how many eons — we dare not guess — what did you do when you got ready to go further? Turned in upon yourself; correct? And this (left hand) needs to get this (right hand) the message to do the same. So what it does is they collapse time. Now they're one, are they not? And when they contemplate, they're not contemplating the seventh heaven any longer; they're contemplating the next heaven (sixth level) because they have already lived the seventh heaven.

They contemplate the seventh heaven (open your hands), but the program is to go out here ( pull them out a step further). Now we're in the sixth reality. What is different about this (sixth) heaven and this (seventh) heaven? (Put the hands together again, showing a greater distance.) Excellent. Is the time slower or faster in the sixth heaven? Slower.

So now if you lived in the sixth reality, how fast would it take from the point that you conceived the thought to the reality happening? (The hands are opened two spaces then brought together.) That's it. Now would you say you're a little slower than the person who lived in the seventh reality? Yes. That's the difference.

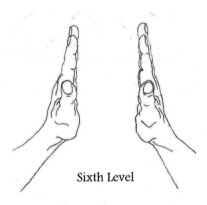

Sixth Level

Now we have a wonderful thing happening here. We have levels. First we have the seventh and now we have the sixth. Notice that the distance between the sixth heaven is longer than the distance between the seventh heaven. How many of you see that? Well, that's the secret of time we are going to talk about. It happens to be the relationship in consciousness, not coagulated points like a distant star. It is consciousness.

Now we have true creation going on. We have the Void and from the Void, inside of the Void, we have Consciousness and Energy that have learned a secret: turn in upon yourself and contemplate. When you do, you become expanded. So now we have a ladder being built.

And we have this mirror consciousness here (right hand) always reflecting to the God consciousness here (left hand). What exists between the two are called potentials of life. So the seventh heaven had a different reality than the sixth heaven. Do you agree?

I want you to now recreate the picture. I want you to draw Point Zero like you've done. This is your godhead. I want you to drop down and draw another point. Between these two points is the seventh plane. I would like you to do that all the way down until you have eight dots. Participate. Just do this on your Void paper. Now with your hands, put them up and start up here and in front of yourself gauge each one of these levels. Come on. Now what level are we on? (Fifth level.) Is the time on this level slower or faster than the sixth level? (Slower.)

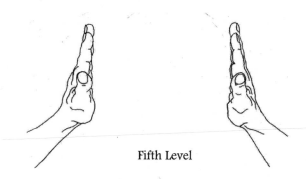

Fifth Level

Now the triad was one of the most holy forms ever created in sacred geometry because the triad maps creation's thoughts from the essential point of creation. And from this point everything else springs. Triangles, like we are going to draw here, are the principal element in life as Consciousness and Energy on this plane.

So what we're going to do here is determine time by placing horizontal lines to separate each level. And every line that we draw, we make it a little longer than the one that preceded it.

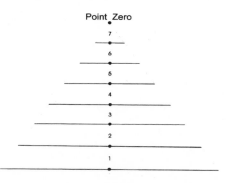

Point Zero

7

6

5

4

3

2

1

Now this looks very simple to you but these are time lines. Today you all exist down here in earth time (first level). You are living in this slow time and on this time line. In this same room we have another level of consciousness existing in another time line in the same space you're occupying except their time is faster than this time. In another, same place you're sitting, we have even a different time line. Its frequency is even more rapid. On and on and on. So where you're sitting is being occupied simultaneously in dimensions by other life forms. The reason you can't see them is because they're vibrating or their energy frequency is much more rapid than the one that you're occupying now. And as far as Earth's magnetics at 8 Hz, you are vibrating at 8 Hz. But a spiritual entity sitting in your midst may be vibrating at 320 Hz.

Now when you were born up at Point Zero, your God created you and you began the journey through contemplation, coming down. You were growing deeper and deeper and deeper in the Void. You were also creating a great linear time from the godhead at Point Zero. Point Zero never moves. Only the mirror consciousness is mobile. When we were in descent, all of us, we called this the Book of Involution. So I want you to draw a line down this side of the pyramid, going down. And I want you to write in your language the word "Involution."

Now how did you get down here? Well, whoever said that this was a bad place? Nobody made you come except yourself. You're the one who wanted to be here. You're the one who made the fall. You're the one who

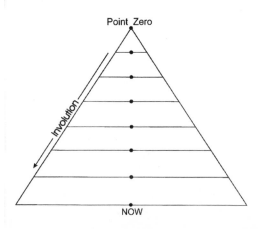

picked up this body and picked up this time line. For eons you have reincarnated into various bodies in order to follow the destiny of this time line through your own exploration.

Now I want to ask you something. You're sitting here vibrating. Look at your hand. Does your hand look the same as your neighbor's hand? Are they as dense as each other's? Well, that means that both of your hands are vibrating at the same rate of speed. Otherwise you couldn't see them if they weren't. Everyone here is the same. Everyone's frequency in the body is the same. Your body's frequency is tied in to this time. Now let me ask you: Just because you're here (first level) and you can't see this (an upper level), does that mean it doesn't exist?

Everything is happening in the shadow of this point and it is all happening within the time and the space that you're sitting in right now. This is an illusion, this time line. This line, right under the center of the pyramid, is called the Now. Where you're sitting is an extraordinary level of intelligence sitting with you. That level of intelligence you can't see because it's vibrating at a greater rate of speed.

Now we're going to do a little demonstration here. Take a colored pencil. And if we know that this is the length of time, if this is consciousness, then it must be energy that is flowing between the two (between each level). I want you to do this, will you. (He draws a wavy line in the seventh level.) Energy undulates like this. This undulation or bell of energy is the oscillation time that it takes from top of curve to bottom of curve. So this is an energy line. I want you to draw those energy lines just like this on the seventh level.

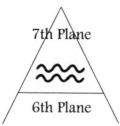

7th Plane

6th Plane

And all that exists is what's between those two points of consciousness. Now what if we close the hands back up. Where does energy go? If there is energy dancing between these two levels of consciousness, when we collapse them where does the energy go? It's collapsed back into consciousness. And when we pull this hand out to the sixth level, what happens to that short wave consciousness that used to exist on the seventh level? Does it still exist? You're learning; just remember you're learning. It still exists.

But now we are sitting in what we call the sixth kingdom. What's happened to the divine energy of the seventh plane? It's winding down; it's curling in on itself. And in the meantime we have this lower wave of energy and a slower time ratio in consciousness creating reality. So if you're living on the sixth level and you once lived on the seventh level, does that mean the seventh level no longer exists? (No.)

Now what I want you to do is study the remainder of this pyramid. And the reason I want you to do this is to learn very simple physics. In doing so you will learn about time, vibrational mass, energy, and why you're here and why you can't see the other planes. I want you to realize that they all exist, but it's a matter of where you bend the focus of your energy. In doing so we will find out why you are here.

What is going to happen to seventh-plane energy that is wound up on the sixth plane? What is going to happen to it when we move it down to the fifth plane? We are pulling it and making it get tighter. Now it becomes the tightened spirals of energy.

What happens to sixth-plane energy? If energy is being wound and tightened down by pulling it to the fifth level, is it going to spring? It is, and it's going to spring around the seventh and sixth energies that have already formed a nucleus.

So what I want you to do is to realize that the energy line from the sixth plane to the fifth plane is a longer time. You will then realize that the energy from the seventh is made into a nucleus and around this nucleus is wrapped the energy of the sixth level. Are you beginning to understand energy and time?

Now you can see what happens to the fourth level. And what happens to the energy and the time of the fifth, sixth, and seventh? They continue to tighten down and wrap around the nucleus until we have atomic structures on the first plane.

So now we have descended all the way to the first plane. What kind of body will you have here? How fast will it vibrate? (Very slow.)

Now what is the reason for the body? The reason is this: that if you are a spiritual being you can only inhabit a plane if you are clothed in elements of that plane. In other words, if the Spirit is born of the Void, then in order for it to exist in a level of time it has to clothe itself in a garment that is made of that time.

# Human Evolution

So here we started out with the first human beings on Earth that used to have two moons and a cloud cover. Your body was not tall, beautiful, and flawless. It was humped over, hairy, and had a small brain. But that hominid entity was the first body of a consciousness coming here that knew only how to get here but nothing about here. Because what is to know about this place other than what one creates about it? Do you understand?

So now here you are on the first plane. You're at the end. Something wonderful starts to happen at the end. Take this consciousness (the right hand) and do this: It starts to swing. This swinging is like a pendulum.

If the consciousness swings out here (to the front), let's say that is a dream. So we are dreaming, yes.

Dreaming

We pause right here (in the middle, parallel to the left hand). This is called the Now alignment. In order for this dream to become real, it has to be lined up with Point Zero.

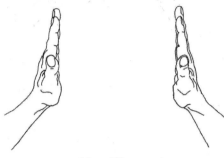

Now Alignment

So now this little entity (right hand) got to swinging around. It's called the mirror consciousness that dreams (forward), aligns (center), moves off (backward), allows it to coagulate and then moves into the coagulation as an experience. (Swinging hand forward, center, backward, center, etc.)

This is necessary because without the mirror consciousness swinging, it cannot imagine. When it moves off center, it can imagine. Once it's created the dream, it lines the dream up, closes the gap into God, pulls back, and programs the dream into reality.

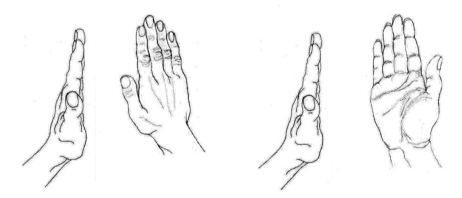

The Dreaming Process

Now who were you? These wonderful, humble creatures that today you would find appalling that you once were. But that's all you needed to be. And how were you to be a part of the Earth that you helped create? How can a Spirit smell a rose? How can a Spirit handle a serpent? How can a Spirit, as it were, be a tree, observe the tree? The entity who chose to come down here, you, came into a body that was made in the same frequency of this Earth with a very small brain. You only needed a little brain, because what did you know? Not a lot. And your face was very large, animallike. Why? Because the eyes had to be large, the nostrils large, the jaw large, the limbs long because this was the body or the vehicle for exploration. To be able to see a tree or touch a tree, to be able to smell flora and pick flora with the body, all that was needed was a very small brain and large senses. Now those were your first bodies.

What is the importance of having this body? Why are you stuck in it? Why can't you get out of it? And once you get out of it, how is it you avoid coming back to it? You don't ever avoid coming back to it. You will always have this body until you have developed your spiritual capacities beyond that which is termed the level of the body.

Now how does a person evolve? How do you change? How did your bodies change to be those beautiful entities they are today from that which is termed their original ancestors? Know how you changed? With the Spirit of Consciousness and Energy flowing through an ancient brain. That brain was able to see only what it knew existed. Every time you ran into a tree, every time you fell off of a rock and every time you experienced Tyrannosaurus Rex and his hot breath, you grew. Every time that you wanted to run for your life and you couldn't run fast enough and you wished that you could, you were changing that which is termed cell biology. What do you think, masters, creates the imprint on your chromosomes? What is your DNA? How does it know how to make you? Who's responsible for putting it together? Do you think your mother and father are responsible for putting you together? They were on an unconscious level. Because, you see, every thought you ever thought, every fear you've ever had, every desire that you've ever had, every betrayal, every feeling, every joy, every moment that you're experiencing it, it is emotion that imprints the DNA. And it is emotion that changes the DNA coil. How does it change it? It imprints it.

So in your first life, if you couldn't run fast enough to get rid of Tyrannosaurus Rex and you'd been consumed by this entity, your last thoughts would be that you wished you would have had longer legs. So you die and your body is swallowed up. It becomes the dung of the Earth and you move to this level here (third level). When you move to this level here all you can remember in viewing your life were all the things that you had learned on this time line and then it stops. That's what you get to see up here in the light (third level).

Now why did you get to come back and what made a difference in your life? You got to come back down here on the time line because the child from the woman you impregnated the night before will be born with longer legs and will genetically pass those on to generations to come. So what you want to come back with is all that you've gained up to this point. That's a very spiritual matron, isn't it?

Most people think in their last dying breath that they're sorry for all the things that they did and they wished they hadn't been so hard on the people that they loved. Indeed they wish they could have been kinder, more giving, more understanding. They have a lot of reflection on the point of death. But that is only as a result of their evolution. The entity that was eaten by Tyrannosaurus Rex had no such reflection. The only reflection that creature had was that it wished it could have outrun the monster. Now that's the last thing it desired.

Up here at the light in its review the entity will see how far it came on the time line. So what is the entity saying to its God? Not that "I'm sorry that I was such an awful child" but it "wished that I had longer legs." And what will your God do? That desire becomes the next generation. So you're born, not into someone with short legs but into a family with long legs. Now we have a Spirit who just wants to run faster than the beasts that are chasing it.

And now it's given a body that genetically gives that potential.

So now this being grows up, outruns, is more clever than the predators around it, because it fathers a next generation that will be exactly what he was in his life emotionally. How many of you understand? He is going to bear children whose life and bodies are going to be better equipped to live in the environment that they are born in. And the souls and Spirits that inhabit those bodies will be entities that have deserved that point in evolution.

Don't you bear today both genetic and emotional traits of your parents, yet have no similarities to your parents at all spiritually? This means that if you are dominated by your parents in physical form, if you have inherited your mother's fear and your father's strength or your father's cowardice and your mother's guilt, if you are predisposed to be that way, it's because the body genetically is creating its reality from its giver, meaning its parents. People who are weak-Spirited are subject to this genetic destiny. In other words, like I said at the beginning this morning, their Spirit energy is being consumed by the genetics of the body. The genetics of the body live off the spiritual energy. And the entity who is supposed to be here to learn has learned nothing.

Now imagine ten and a half million years. How long do you live: 60 years, 70 years, 100 years? How many lifetimes, at an average of 80 years, can be lived in ten and a half million years? A lot. You know, entities say you're an old soul or you're a young soul. No, all souls were created at the same time. Do you think you have only lived two lives? There is no one in here that has lived two lives. You have lived thousands of them.

Now does it make logical sense that your forefathers and foremothers, who were apelike in appearance, evolved Homo erectus — the hominids evolved to Homo erectus — and then from Homo erectus to Neanderthal. Is there a reason why these creatures changed? What was the reason? Why did you change? What made you change?

Did people evolve because people had adversity? Did people evolve because they had problems? Haven't you evolved in this lifetime because of the difficulties you went through? So be it.

Now is it fair then to say that your forefathers and foremothers had a lot of difficulties and they had a lot of problems? Well, you should then because you are the product of their resolve, what you are today. You came from the godhead and you have a mandate. And the mandate says, "Make known the unknown." That is the only law there is. Make known the unknown. That is what the Void said to its creation here, "Make of me whatever you want. Be the creator. I give you whatsoever you desire. There is no right or wrong; there is only evolution. There is only creativity."

Therefore, we have learned that the original entity, though as powerful as it was, had to move all over the Void to finally realize that it had gone nowhere. And we now call this entity God. And God has most certainly evolved from those days. Now God has a coherent life form, and God has a coherent vacuum of time. Indeed this is the playground in which we are to fulfill the law of "Make known the unknown." When we first came into our bodies, you and I, we didn't know anything other than what we had gained in previous incarnations in this time flow (Earth time). If this were our first lifetime, we would know nothing. And all we had to teach us was our environment and the adversity of our environment and the need, as it were, of being trapped in the physical body, to survive in that body.

But after the first lifetime we started learning. And what were we contributing to this life line? We were contributing thought. We were endowed with a mechanism that could take a stream of consciousness because, remember, consciousness, the brain and the mind, are all different. Consciousness is the stream of God. The brain is the receiver, for it takes that consciousness and creates it into memorable neurological thought and it can freeze that thought in the form of memory. Memory in creation is like gathering blocks of stone in which to build a hovel. Thought in the brain, collected in the form of knowledge, allows you to recreate thought forms, that if they are held in the forefront of the brain's neocortex will be the lawgivers that collapse energy into form. So the brain had to evolve to fit our level of need.

Now what are we gaining out of this? If we realize that we need longer legs to outrun Tyrannosaurus Rex, that would be a learning. That is creation, just the need through adversity to be better. Therein lays the groundwork of the body for a more evolved body. What does it do for your spiritual self? It has made you realize that in order to live here you must recreate yourself. Here on the earth plane we have lived ten and a half million years. You have all been children, fathers, mothers, sistern, and brethren. You have all been slain, eaten, burned, died peacefully, drowned. You have all met your death in a myriad of uncreated ways. You've done it all.

455,000 years ago, approximately, something wonderful happened. While you were still on the seventh level, other beings were already descending. You see, no one descended at the same time; everyone went differently. And yet it was up to each one of you to create according to your desire. You still have beings today that are alive and well on the fifth plane and they have never gone any lower. Perhaps in the next two hundred years they'll make their way down to the Earth level; perhaps they'll never come. But that's all they have known. Some of you call them angels. You call them that because they have an utter innocence about this place. They have no judgment, no good and bad. They understand it not. They only understand love. But they have never lived here. They have never been a Christ because they have never embodied God in flesh and blood.

While you were still on the seventh level, we already had entities that had come down to the first plane billions and billions of years ago who were on this time line in this three-dimensional matter vibrating at 8.2 Hz. They had already moved down the time line. Now when they had moved past the center line, they were already building a spiritual reality that was moving way up to the fourth level. In other words, their reality was happening this fast (fourth level) in a body this slow (first level). Do you understand?

On the time line they started gradually getting brighter and brighter, and they exist about the fourth level. They are your brothers and sisters. They live on various different planets and most of them live on the interior of those planets, since all orbiting orbs are hollow. They surpass you now. 455,000 years ago every one of you in this room came up against this

time line; you finally got this far. So how far were you? Well, you knew
you were male and female. You would cohabitate for the sake of bearing
young. The females were dominant in the tribes, since they were that which
is termed the culture's leaders. The males provided the food for the family.
We had sort of a moral household.

At this particular point this group of entities that came before you, called
the Gods, came back. They came down here and they realized, "Hey, you
need a little help" because you hadn't advanced very far. So what did they
do? They mercifully interacted in your time line of evolution.

You possessed a small brain and large facial features. This small brain
ended up being the reptilian brain and the midbrain up to the corpus
callosum. So in other words the brain did not contain the neocortex. At this
point in your evolution you were very psychic. You could send messages far
and wide because your brain operated in infrared, which is called the psychic
realm, but you still had a primitive brain. These entities came along, took
you and commingled their seed with yours, and bred into your body their
experiences.

Remember I asked if you wore your parents' identity as well as their
emotional identity. When these elected beings finished commingling with
all of you, you drastically changed as a culture. Not only did you start to
lose body hair but you gained in proportional height. Your skeleton changed.
You lost two ribs and gained an enormous brain. Your facial features became
less defined than the overexaggerated hominid's facial features.

Now why did they do this? Because they are your brothers and sisters.
They are Gods from the same Source who are ahead of you in evolution.
They also used you as servants, which would make a great amount of logic
since you didn't know all that they knew.

So what were your tasks? Your tasks were to commingle, cohabitate,
and to live with them. They in turn taught you psychology. They taught you
art. They taught you mathematics, astronomy. It was they who imbued within
you a sense of culture and, moreover, a sense of that which is termed
dynamic self. But how great were you? You had a large neocortex, large,

but barely used because the experience that it took to give you that genetic body, as a Spirit, you have not lived. So it would be as if your children were walking around in their parents' clothing. The clothing fits but it is still a child who is exhibiting itself in the body. Do you understand? Now that happened 455,000 years ago.

Those Gods who became the legends of biblical texts created your bodies, created my body, interacted, and went on about their life. What did it do for all of us? What it did is that it brought us to a holding pattern on the time line. You haven't changed. You have been reincarnating over and over and over again, coming back with the same amount of spiritual growth as you left behind the last lifetime. Now what is that to say? That humanity leveled off 40,000 years ago, and the cranium of the human being from 40,000 years ago to today hasn't changed. So it means that as spiritual people you keep reincarnating into a genetic line that you still have yet to use all of its machinery.

Are you learning anything? Now this seems that this introduction is very tedious, but it can be somewhat interesting when you begin to understand where your roots go back. And it is important for you to understand this before you can go on and start creating reality. You need some answers to your questions. You don't use all of your brain. You use less than a tenth of it. Less than a tenth of the massive neocortex means that there is a great deal of potential that you have never actualized. Even Einstein when he perished had not used all of his brain. He had not mapped that which is termed new ideas and new theories and fell short of developing the discovery of new mathematics to describe what he was seeing in a unified vision.

So if you are a spiritual being who is actually behind nature, it would then begin to make a great deal of logic to you that the laziness inside of you and the impatience inside of you are a primitive Spirit in a very advanced body. Does that make logic to you? And the reason you haven't evolved a great deal in ten and a half million years is because you're still back 455,000 years ago and you have yet to use the capacity of your body. You have yet to develop your spiritual self so that it can operate this body as a fine-tuned instrument of God.

Now what did you do last lifetime? Were you in the technical revolution? Did you die in World War II? Was your home bombed? Did you die of famine in Ireland? Did you die of the plague? How many children did you have and where are they today? What did you contribute last lifetime? Can't remember.

In this life and why you came here to learn was "How do I live to the greatest of my spiritual potential thereby using my body to its greatest potential?" And do you have Gods in your genes? Indeed you do. Do you have an advanced intelligence that you're carrying around in you? Indeed you do. Are you the children of a superior race? Many of them. But the race itself is only as great as the intelligence that created it, and that of course comes back to God, the dreamer of all origins.

At this time the reason that you are unhappy with your life is because you are at the end of your ability to dream reality; you let everything else do it for you. You go to the motion pictures and you let someone else act out an adventure while you stand by and watch. You listen to someone else sing you a melody while your mouth stays quiet. You swoon at someone else's poetry. You marvel at someone else's artwork. You let someone else's genius plug you in, for convenience. Is it any wonder you are bored and need entertainment? Because it is not coming out of you.

If you are Gods, and you most certainly are, and if Consciousness and Energy create the nature of reality, perhaps the problem that we have here is the inability to believe in one's self or its capability. And perhaps you have inherited that gene through your parents. Most parents never believed they were greater than the stock from which they came.

So here's what you've been doing for 40,000 years. You have had this consciousness out here swinging violently back and forth. How fickle are you? Do one moment you approve and the next moment you disapprove? Is one moment you like and the next moment you don't like? And what about your future? What future? Oh, that future. Isn't your future just more of thinking about your past? Well, if that's so, then your future is stuck in the past.

And so someone told you that God no longer existed inside of you but was separate from you. When the Gods left, they went to heaven and they left you here. And you believed that. And so belief, being the creator of reality, put to bed this God-in-you and separated you from the God of your choice.

What about Jehovah? Jehovah is nothing more than an advanced entity who was highly insecure, warlike, and who hated his sister. How about the Lord God Id? They were Gods, beings, people, that have problems just like you're having problems. But somewhere they told you that they were Lord and someone got it mixed up that Lord meant "boss."

And so the God that you're supposed to line up with, create a dream and give it to, and then move off of that dream so it can manifest in energy and bring the experience, got stuck because you think it's out there instead of within you. So for 40,000 years you've been doing this same thing every lifetime. And what does that mean? That means that you've gone to school and you've learned everything that the culture has to give you and you're bored and you have nothing else to contribute because you don't know how to dream the dream, line it up, collapse time, bring it back, have energy collapsed into visual form, and then experience it.

So now we live in lack, which needs to stop. We have everyone moving a little bit down the time line, then they die, go up to the light, take a look at their life review, and return back to this time line. You're stuck. No one can get past their image. Only a few are breaking away and going beyond. And as they get past this "God problem" they start to become spiritual, and they're reaching deep within the Source and manifesting it on the first plane. Who is a Christ? One who finishes the time line and goes home.

# IV.
## Energy for Dreaming

## Runners

I n the deliverance of that which is termed this philosophy, I am sending you "runners" to help manifest it for you so that you see it as a truth. So be it. Now what's a runner? An entity who brings your past is a runner; an entity who rings your phone is a runner. Someone who is interacting with you or creating a situation in which the result of that interaction brings forth a specific philosophy that can be experienced in truth is a runner. Now I am going to send you a lot of runners. The only reason that I am giving you what I am giving you today is that this year in your time is leading up to some quite marvelous discoveries. And when they happen, you will remember reading these words. And I dare say you will be looking for your papers and pencils and you'll be grabbing someone to draw these little pictures — time lines and such.

## Energy Waves

Now we are going to talk about energy. Energy is related to knowledge that is represented in the serpent. It is called that because that is what a wave of energy looks like. Now energy doesn't just start and then end. It begins with a thought and ends with a thought. Two levels of consciousness contain energy.

Now energy undulates. According to whatever level of consciousness is being extracted into the experience tells us what kind of energy to expect. If we have a very advanced intelligence, if we have that which is termed an advanced level of consciousness, then what you start to feel from them are bursts of advanced, powerful energy. Moreover, entities who have the ability to manifest their thoughts have this sort of energy radiating from them. If we have entities who are slow and slothlike, who are definitely on this first level time line, who don't care very much about life, their energy is going to be like long, undulated energy, preceded and ending with thoughts and conclusions.

Well, what does this mean, this wave line? When you say that an entity has wonderful energy, what do you mean when you say that? Or what do you mean when you say, "I felt a very harmful energy coming off of that person." Have you made such statements in your life?

Now that means that energy is a virgin but it is a carrier wave of thought; it is thought in motion. So if a person has a very harmful energy, you'll feel it because it is their consciousness flowing through their brain emanating in the form of a mind. And that mind rides this field. And you pick it up in your lower cerebellum/subconscious mind, the portion of the brain that deciphers energy into fields of collective thought. In other words, it weighs it. Is this good or is this bad? Good or bad? Energy is neither good nor bad. Energy is neither positive nor negative; it's both. And nothing is good or bad as seen in the light of all eternity. But in order for you to be creators and Gods, like I said that you are, then there must be something in you that would ring forth a divineness. In other words, there's got to be something more than digestion that seems to equate to your divine nature. So what is it?

There is a saying that is vastly underused and misused, and it's called that which is hidden. That which is hidden is sacred knowledge. But what is that sacred knowledge? The sacred knowledge is that until you can uncover that which is hidden, you will never gain the sacred knowledge. But in a philosophical commentary on that, we would say then that that which is hidden simply means that inside every wave of energy is a carrier field of mind, and that energy is both a particle and a wave and that it starts with an idea or a thought. When it is released, it is moved into a field and concludes as reality.

So look at the space between you or an object or another person in the room. Just turn around and gauge the space between the two of you. What is existing in that space? Can you feel its energy? Is it dead or alive? What is it that you're not seeing? What about between you and I? What about this space? This space is called that which is hidden. It is the invisible. And the invisible simply says that this atmosphere around you is a field of energy that looks just like this and that in this field of energy we have energy and potentials.

Now as far as it takes to touch the object or person is the only distance required to go back to the seventh level. Everything that you want in your life — fabulous wealth, radiant youth, health, longevity, the energy that it takes to bring that about in your life — takes less of a field than it takes to touch this object or person. So do it again and contemplate that which is hidden.

Now the atmosphere in linear time, the atmosphere in the room, those fields that make up the elements of the Earth, solar system, and the galaxy are all made up of the same energy field in different stages of evolution. But it is the same field in different stages.

Now what is divine in you? What is divine in you is Consciousness and Energy being frozen through the mechanics of a human brain. Why is that important? Because if you are surrounded with this potential Consciousness and Energy, and you must be surrounded with these potentials, then what is it that affects this field? Thought. It's called the observer. And where is the observer? The observer is inside your head.

Now if you have the power to create reality it means you have the power to affect the quantum field. And what is in this field is all of Consciousness and Energy (thoughts) in different stages all the way up the triad. And what is it about you that can affect the field? Every time your brain reaches a neurological conclusion that sits in the frontal lobe, it changes the field to reality. You don't know it, but it does. Whenever you are having a thought, you are affecting the field around you.

How do you do that? All matter, all mass, what you're sitting on, what you're wearing, what your body is made up of, is made up of subatomic particles. Have you heard of atoms? Do you not find it interesting that atoms and Adam sound the same — the first man, the first particle? What do you think an atom looks like? It has a nucleus; correct? What is composed in the nucleus? Protons. What else? What is inside a proton? A quark. So where did they come from? Right here (sixth level) is the quark field. Down here (fifth level) is the proton field. Down here (third level) is the closure of the nucleus, and all down here (first and second levels) is the racing of matter and antimatter, what are called electrons and positrons. So all an atom is is the availability of potential.

If you unfurl an atom at its nucleus level, you have an atomic bomb. How many of you know the power of an atomic bomb? Isn't it interesting that the energy comes from that which is hidden? The smaller the particle, the more powerful the energy. Did it ever occur to you, beginners, where that energy came from? Perhaps the energy that is unfurled in the splitting of the nucleus is really splitting apart this coiled energy that has been tightened down through the slowing of time. Does that make logic to you? Is that a nice philosophy? Because if you rupture it, the kind of energy that you get is the sort of energy that is common on these levels.

And that's what an atom is. All it is is that which is hidden of seven levels of reality in a particle. Now what affects the atom? If all matter is all made up of atoms, how did it get there? All an atom is is atmospheres of other planes coagulated and closed. Are they sensitive? Well, if we have a nucleus and then we have the outer shell and we have orbiting electrons and positrons, that then means that every electron that moves around this atom moves around this atom because we allow it to move around the atom. And how is it that we allow? We take it for granted. In other words, you're the observer. If you focused on this particular particle, this atom, if you focused on its electrons, you could reverse the spin on the electrons of this atom. Why can you do that? Because that is your divine nature. If you're supposed to evolve and make known the unknown, what is the faculty in you that is responsible for doing it? It is focused consciousness. When you have a thought and if you were to focus on this atom by adding electrons or taking them away, you would change the nature of its energy.

The field that exists between you and I, you don't see. And you don't see it because it's in motion, momentum. At the moment you stop to look at the atmosphere between you and I, you start to see little lights. How many of you have seen those? You have? And someone told you that was just something happening with your eyeball? That's not anything happening with your eyeball. Those little lights are, in effect, this energy wave collapsing into a particle with an orbital light, which is called the electron. The moment you stop focusing on the invisible field, the lights disappear. Then all you see is what you're looking at in the near distance, you to I, I to you.

As long as you ignore this field, it stays inert, meaning you don't activate it so it stays status quo. The moment that you focus on what is hidden, you unveil what is hidden.

Now Consciousness and Energy create the nature of reality. Any solid object is made solid by the creator of that object. And the creator of that object agrees that it is solid so it stays solid. But the truth is when you go to sleep tonight your bedroom will disappear, or it will fuzz out, and the light in your refrigerator will fade because the moment you go to sleep, you are no longer observing your room. And the moment you no longer observe your room, it fuzzes out. Do you agree? It's the way it is.

Now how is it you can open one little eyelid and gaze around the room and see everything the way it's supposed to be? Who determines that it's going to be that way? You are correct. But what if one morning you woke up and saw that you were in the twenty-third universe? What would happen to your room?

Well, it depends, you see. This is a trap. Because if you woke up thinking you were in the twenty-third universe and knew absolutely that you were there, you would be there. It would be very clear. The moment you asked yourself, "What happened to my room?" you'd wake up. You got it?

Now you're so powerful that whatever you put in your frontal lobe, no matter if it's trash or divinity, it affects energy. Whatsoever you think is either freeing energy up from its past or collapsing it into its future. When we allow energy to be, it moves and undulates. What happens when we focus on it? It becomes mass. What happens when we forget about it? Party time. It goes back to its wave movement. This is the way it works.

On the first plane you have a fabulous atmosphere of all these potentials, but what happens? The reason people stay on the same time lines incarnation after incarnation after incarnation is because they have given their focused, conscious power over to the needs of their body. And they are born into a body that is genetically predisposed to be a certain way. And so they allow the body to grow up and have its way. The body is on genetic automatic pilot. Are you still with me?

Now as long as the body is on automatic pilot, everything is set for your life. Nothing is moving in and out of it; it's all set. So you go day-in and day-out allowing your body to create reality. Now what does your body know about creating reality? It knows only to survive and that it needs food to survive and that it needs sleep and that it needs to be urinated. It needs to have its waste removed from it and after a rest it's rejuvenated. That is called survival.

Most people, although highly educated, never get beyond the level of survival in their life. They never move into the free space of creativity so magic, as it is termed, never happens to them. If the body or the brain is operating on a day-to-day life, then what is tomorrow going to bring? You know what tomorrow is going to bring because you've lived millions of tomorrows, so your tomorrow is just your past. If you go to school and you learn all of this knowledge, it is just memorized theory. And the only reason that you learn that is so that you can make a living to feed your body. Do you understand?

If you are magnetically attracted to another person and you may never have been ever attracted to this Spirit before, why are you attracted to this body type? Because the body type is equal to the body type and complements the one that you have. There is a magnetic resonance involved. So you have relationships and you have copulation and you bear children. What kind of children are you going to have? You're going to have children that are slightly improved from you. But are they born with an ability to intuitively create? Or are they needing to be educated in order to create?

So now how many lives do you think you've lived like this to where you've allowed your body to dictate your life? Infinite.

Why is magic so important? Because magic never happens openly to those who are living a life dictated by their genetics. Why? Because it is the observer in us, it is the Spirit in us, that has the power to reveal what is hidden, not the body. But if we are weak and live only for our material self, we never develop the focus necessary to unveil the distance between you and I into a reality.

So you want to get away from this life? You think it is so terrible? It is a blessing. Because no matter if you die tonight, you are going to be born back into this existence. And what kind of parents are you going to come back to? Those that are equal to your level of acceptance now. So then you are going to be born again. This body and this brain are going to die, and all of its cognitive memory will perish with it. Then you will be in a brand new body that you have to develop again and are a little bit uncertain about its genetic programming.

You won't remember this life. And you think this is bad and you want to get out of this life, but you are just jumping into another fire. You know how many times you've been doing it? For eons. Let us say safely that you have been on a static progress for 40,000 years. And so who is responsible for all of this technology? A few people. And why did they bring about such technology? Because those beings had an ability that you will learn. You're going to be inspired and you will develop. It is the ability of imagination, to take knowledge and put it together in building blocks of thoughtful creativity and then to be possessed of that thought. If you are possessed of such an imagination for a period of time and your level of acceptance is that you accept it, then that thought will affect this field. What was will dissolve and will begin to move into a liquid state. Imagination will reaffect this state and it will coagulate, not as it used to be but what it will be.

Spiritual people are the people who have led discovery. Spiritual people have been the philosophers of old that have given to you and your generations the groundwork of a philosophy that always talks about what is hidden within the individual. And it has only been a few sparkled through every civilization that have made an impact on the culture as a whole.

But you were not responsible for the microchip; you were not responsible for the physics of the microchips. You were not the creator of rupturing the nucleus of an atom. Nor were you the entity who created telepathic uses in the form of a telephone. You did not create the microwave. You did not create the television. You did not create the auto machine. You did not weave the carpet that you are sitting upon. So what did you do? You worked for them.

Now when we wake up consciously there comes a moment that we know. I had my moment and you'll have yours. In that moment we are suddenly separated from our ignorance and uplifted into a mist of freedom;

it's called knowingness. The moment that you know that your focused thought affects life, when you really know, that is the moment that you will start to take care, to discipline your thinking. If the Spirit is awakened in you, it will liberate you. Joy is not being physical. Joy is being the lord of the physical, not its slave.

So if you've created everything in your life, people, you're responsible for everything you've done for yourself. You're responsible for your successes and your failures, and it was you who determined if they were a success or a failure. If you are the person responsible for your happiness or your depression, it was you who chose to feel those ways. And it was as simple as that and always has been.

The moment that you know that your mind can shift from the past of limited thinking and accelerate unlimited thought, your life changes in that moment. And how does it change? It says, "Now I know that the power was within me. Whatsoever I think, I create. My reality is only equal to my runaway thinking. But what if I were to sit still for one moment and ask myself: What want I from this life? What is it that I have never known? What is it I have never experienced? What about myself? If I use less than a tenth of my brain, what must I do to activate the rest of it? And what far potential would I possess if indeed I could do that?

Now you make a list. What would you want to do? If your life could be longer and you could change anything according to what you're thinking and according to your acceptance, how different would you be today? Vastly different, vastly different. Because in that moment then you would understand that the brain operates on flashes of pictures, holograms, and that every time they flash, we call this thinking. And that every time it flashes, it occupies the frontal lobe. And every time it flashes from this point, it's affecting this field and creating those thoughts.

What if then I could draw a thought and what if I could hold that thought for a deliberate period of time? Would the same law apply to a deliberate use of the observer's principle in creating reality? Indeed it will.

93

Because the moment you hold it with utter acceptance is the moment you change your time line. Everything starts to change into a flux.

What you dream, what you hold in a focused thought, will allow past realities to dissolve. Your life will start to fall apart. And you will say, "This is not what I saw." Yes, it is what you saw. Because as everything falls apart, what we are saying is if we could dismantle the particles of a table, the table would disappear and what we would have would be a radiant light field where the table once was. The light field then changes into our new thought as reality. That's change, is it not?

So how constricted is your life? The life that you've had on the time line has been stuck and keeps reincarnating itself. What is beyond this place? Is there more to live, more to be, more to know? There is indeed. But what must you do to get in the time line? You have to dissolve the past, because everyone in this room thinks in terms of their future based on their past. And what holds you there? Guilt, negativity, fear, and afraid to change.

What happens when you focus on something wonderful in your life? A lot of things in your life are going to fall apart. Why? Because the energy that holds them together must be liberated so that what you are wanting can be reformed.

This is enough for this day. I want to end this day in saying to you what you have long heard but never understood: God is love. What does that mean? Say it to yourself. What does that mean? Love is the act of always giving. It's not about taking. God gives and holds steadfast the principle of life that it can be explored.

When you love yourself, it will not be an impassioned embrace. It will not be about consoling yourself with poetic words. What is love is the act of giving. To give. God never takes, only gives. Life has been expanded from this moment; it's never been contracted. God is incapable of judgment. God is incapable of judging you, hating you, condemning you. There is no such thing. There is only allowing.

To know what love is is to open up and to give. It is like breaking down the dam of water that is held back by the dam; it is a giving of consciousness. When you learn to love yourself, you will learn to love yourself as such. You will give to yourself not things, but freedom. You will cease judging yourself as being a failure or a success. You will cease feeling guilty about your past because you never have a future as long as you are anchored in guilt. You will give up your enemies because when you give them up, they give you up. That is loving yourself. It takes an enormous amount of energy to have an enemy and to keep them always in your mind.

Loving yourself is forgiving you. And say to yourself, "In the light of all eternity, what was this action worth? Was it worth holding me back forever? Or can I expand myself so I can see over the hill?" God is love because God gives you every day of your life and supports you with the energy necessary to create life. And you have your time and you have your season. When you can do the same with yourself, then love is born in you.

Don't expect people to love you; they are incapable of it. Expect yourself to love you. And the way you love you is to give to you freedom, peace. And when you take that and give it to yourself, you then usher it to other people. Give to them. Give to them.

Give people room to make mistakes. So what? They're on the verge of wisdom. Virtue is not the abstinence in life; it's doing it in life. Give people a wide berth. Don't look for them to make a mistake. Love them; allow them. Don't hold someone in your power and play games with them. Give them freedom and be honest and truthful with them. And the honesty is, "I am giving to you what I most crave in myself." Forgive your parents if they didn't raise you properly. No one knows how to raise anyone properly. Celebrate that you have life and that your parents gave you life.

Give. Give. Don't take. Don't take. Give, and in the act of giving you become God. When you are merciful, your God is merciful. When you are forgiving, your God is forgiving. How can you expect to forgive yourself and not forgive your enemies? Only when you have forgiven yourself do you have the wisdom to enact that power towards others.

People who are takers are victims; and you've all been takers. You think life owes you something. You think your parents owe you something. You think your friends owe you something. You think your lover owes you something. No one owes you anything. You're a taker, not a giver. If you're a taker then you do not embody God. If you're a giver you embody the divine power within you because there is no end to the resource.

I want you to sit down and think of three things that you would like to have happen in your life, just three things: A dream; it can be anything. It can be a more glorious Spirit. It can be having lucid life as lucid dreaming. It can be fabulous wealth. It can be anything as long as you accept it. Now if you don't accept what you're putting down, you shall not have.

So go back into your room of dreams and go look for something you lost along the way. Most of you lost it when you were children. Go back and find something that you would like to have happen to you. But make certain it's within the realm of your acceptance.

Then you write them out; draw a picture of each one. When you are finished with these three, I want you to contemplate yourself. Then I want you to focus on what you want you to change about yourself. Remember, everything is possible. There is no such thing as permanent addiction to the past. It's only temporary.

You focus on your lack, your doubt, anything, your sickness, and write it out. What are the three things you want to change about your life? Write them out and then draw a picture of each of these three. That's all I want you to do.

Then before you go to your slumber, don't watch television; read, so that you go to sleep with lofty thoughts in your mind. And what is it you need to read? Read about quantum mechanics. Read about creating reality. Read about the concept of another life and who you will be in that other life. Give yourself food for your Spirit; not your body but your Spirit. And go to sleep with that in your brain. And you're going to change by tomorrow. And you will feel lifted. That's part of the journey. That's how it starts.

Now I love you. How is it I can do that? Because I give to you. And what is there about you to love? That which I was. You are forgotten Gods, utterly. You are in a state of amnesia about your own divinity. You are, for the most part, superstitious and dogmatic.

What I have taught you is very simple. It is most certainly complex when we understand it in biological terms. And it may be disturbing and complex when we talk about the hidden being made manifest as energy. But it will become clear.

There is a lot you don't know. Do not guard your ignorance so jealously. I certainly would not put up barriers of doubt to keep my ignorance intact.

So be open-minded. I love you. You've already done the worst you can do to yourself. There is nothing worse than you've already done. And you will never be possessed or cultlike, nor will you be a follower, nor will you be brainwashed. You have already been that. You will never go backwards; you will only go forwards.

So be it.

I salute the God within you.

# V.
## How I Teach

I salute you from the Lord God of my being to the Lord God of your being. Let's have a drink.

O my beloved God,
That which has created me
And given unto me life,
Awaken in me
My passion to know.
Give back my power,
That I may manifest
A journey,
A path,
To enlightenment.
So be it.
To life.

To be that which is termed God within is to be light of heart, light, joyful; not artificially joyful, but an ease about life instead of a burden about it.

Now listen. One fine morning you will wake up and realize, as it were, what I have taught you. And you won't sit there struck dumb. You'll start laughing. It shall come from some wonderful place. And you're going to laugh and laugh and laugh because you will see the mirth that lies on the other side of a serious human attitude that everything is oppressive and everything is dreadful. I tell you the God that I love never judged anyone. It's a giving entity; it's a source. It never says to you, "Well, you want it but you can't have it." It never says to you, "You should do penance before you will get it." It never says to you, "You should say you're sorry; then I'll give it to you." They should take Yeshua ben Joseph off of that cross. What a sad sight. It is to make you feel guilty.

I tell you the God that you're learning about is everlasting life and a life that is so full that you don't even have the mind yet to begin to recognize how much there is yet to experience. Don't you know that you have experienced the most rotten part of life? If you're stuck in a reincarnation loop, you have been living the same attitude. Just imagine, imagine you sitting here. Imagine a thousand lifetimes being the same you in different bodies. How boring. No wonder you're not invited back home.

Your ability to change is in a moment. Imagine what you have not learned. Imagine what you don't know. You've been stuck, reincarnated on the same behavioral pattern. Different bodies; same old attitude. You can't do any worse than you've already done. You know, there are some entities who say that all you will learn with life is not worth anything and it's all right to kill and all that stuff. Let me tell you something: If you've been alive or been coming back here for the last ten and a half million years, don't you think that the probability that you've already created such atrocities is fairly great? I would suggest that it's probably the odds of ten and a half million to one that you have already murdered someone else and then, of course, been murdered, and that you've been scoundrels, derelicts. You've been rapers, you've been kings and queens, paupers, slaves, servants, holy men, sinful men, virtuous women, whoring women. You've been everything. So what makes you think that what is to know is more of the same stuff? It doesn't get worse after this. It gets greater.

Let's not ponder, as someone else suggested, that everything is all right. Let's not say that this teaching gives you permission to be bad; you've already been bad. What the teaching does is to tell you to realize that and to say, "What are you going to do with the rest of your life?" Are you going to be the same old predictable person every single day so much so that you don't even love yourself? And if you met yourself and yourself asked you to have a relationship, you would run away from yourself.

What are you going to do the rest of your life? What are you going to do? Are you going to continue to work the rest of your life? Are you going to continue to get stoned for the rest of your life? Are you going to continue to live off of other people the rest of your life? Are you going to continue to feel sorry for yourself for the rest of your life? Are you going to make people feel bad about your existence, your mother, your father? What are you going to do? You're going to have children and make them feel bad about being born? What are you going to do until, oh, say, the day you die? What's on your agenda?

The teachings, as a master appropriately replied, give us hope. They give us hope because first it gives us knowledge to put down our ignorance. And don't you know that superstition comes out of ignorance? Think of all the cultures who are superstitious about walking under a ladder. Think of all the cultures that are superstitious about blaspheming God. Think of all the cultures that are superstitious about virginity. Think about all of the cultures that absolutely believe in blood sacrifice. Think about them. The teachings put to rest superstition and ignorance.

What you learn today is that which is termed a marriage of science, theology, and me. You're going to learn practical aspects about your brain, what part responds to what. You're going to get to answer a question of,

"Where do I get the body that I move into after the death of this body? Where does it come from? How do I manifest it?" You will be answering questions to yourself of, "Why are some people psychic and others are not?"

This isn't new knowledge. In fact the new knowledge of today is pitifully impoverished and for the most part is intended to be because governments do not survive when people are all-knowing and aware. Commercialism does not survive when people have the power to create reality. So in this culture there is a downplay of the divinity of man and an intent conspiracy of robbing everyone of individual thought. That's why everyone is intent upon making everyone the same, believe the same, act the same, buy the same products, look the same, because in sameness there is control. In individuality there is unpredictability. Governments must hold themselves together with the populace that they can corner and catalog. And governments only survive as power when everyone agrees. But what if America, this place, were all enlightened to the level of Christ? Would we still have Republicans and Democrats? Would you have a national debt? Would you? Would you have, what is it called, Medicare?

So how about people who have an agenda about keeping a government together? Is it to their advantage to do away with superstition and dogma? It is not to their advantage. It divides and conquers people and they are the people who keep them in control.

Now this teaching is not secular. This teaching is about a brain, a spiritual body, and levels of development. The teaching says to you very blatantly today, "You have in you everything you need to change your life." Now is there someone here, including me, going to make you change? No. You are forgotten Gods. You may be forgotten but you're still Gods. And the only entities that have forgotten that truth is you. So being a God then, and being that you have a responsibility to make known the unknown, you must have your own will. After you learn all the knowledge you learn today, if you do not use it, that is your will. That does not mean you are right or wrong; it is simply your choice. But knowledge frees us from fear, the fear that we can't do the work. And the future suddenly becomes predictable instead of unpredictable.

You don't know if this is the truth. What did I tell you about the truth? Nothing I tell you is the truth. God only knows what you know. And it's only truth when it gets to be in your way and you have to work your way through it. Then it's truth. If it never gets in your way and you never put it there, it will never be truth; it will be just another New Age teaching. It won't be truth until you experience it. And you need a lot of truth in order to stand up to your cynical mind. You do. It doesn't do anyone any good to say, "You have the power to heal yourself," if they don't believe it.

Moreover, it doesn't do any of you any good to say you want to be wealthy. If you want to be wealthy, you must sit down and create a card with a picture of fabulous wealth and focus on it for an hour each day until your focus turns to being it. That's all you have to do. Then you get it. Now what you do with it, that's another focus. But unless you use the discipline, it doesn't work and it's not going to be the truth.

So, no, I don't talk about the truth; I talk about that which is termed a philosophy. It was truth for me and allowed me to emerge in this time frame to give you what I knew. Is it important that you believe in me? You don't have to believe in me; that's not a requirement. What you do need to do is to believe in yourself. And use me. Use me like a burning bush. Listen to what I have to say. Pick and choose out of it what is right for you. And you don't have to use it all. And if it doesn't work, then you can still use me to blame for it not working. I come in very handy in that category.

Do that until you're tired of doing it. Then take your responsibility and say, "Look, if I would have really wanted this, I would have gotten it." That's how it is. Immaculate faith happens in a moment. Immaculate curing, healing, restoration, happens in a moment. And the reason it takes so long for most of you is because the road is paved with doubt and disbelief. Now if you can get rid of that, in a moment everything you want will fall right into place. It takes you that long to manifest it.

You see, you're in slow time (first plane). It takes a long time to manifest in that time line. But what if you had the faith of a seventh-level being? We call those beings masters. They live in a body but their mind is on the seventh level and their energy is on the seventh level, and they use it in a physical body in this time flow. When they say something, it takes only a moment for it to happen. If your consciousness is on the first three planes, and you believe only in your stomach and you believe only in your body and your addictions, you know how long it takes for something to happen? Most of you live here and don't even take the time to focus; too impatient. So you hang out in this time and your time line is slow to produce.

There are people in this school who still haven't manifested what they say they really want. Why? Because that manifestation stays in slow time instead of in mind time. Now they're really wonderful in other areas. They are very unique. In some areas of the teaching they have absolute knowingness that pulls them from this body to a greater consciousness. So with that knowingness, when they focus on something, it doesn't take that long for it to manifest. So they have evolved their consciousness from slow time to fast time. Their mind is developing. But not all of it is developed. A lot of it is still sitting in slow time.

So we have people who can manifest out of thin air an object. But what about telling them to heal themselves? The same person who can manifest out of thin air you would be impressed, and you're going to get to see them. But what if I say to them, "Go over there and heal this person." Suddenly their acceptance moves down into unacceptance. Why do you think that is? Because they accept some things and deny other things. And it's the very thoughts they accept that they manifest straightaway. And it's the very thoughts that they don't accept that they don't get straightaway.

So what about you? I'm saying to you, "Today I will give to you all of this knowledge. You're going to know more about the brain than 99.9% of the people in your country. And you're going to know about seven bodies that nobody knows about. And you're going to leave here today with a discipline and have manifested three things you want and changed three things you want.

If you have moved yourself up to utter acceptance, you get them all immediately. Everything starts to fall apart the day you leave here. It's in shambles. Everything falls apart because the glue that holds your present together is the energy and your focus. The moment you change your focus, it's pulled away and the energy disperses. Relationships start to change; they fire you from your job; your cat bites you on the leg; your bird flies away; your dog has rabies. Everything falls apart.

Now I want you to expect that. You know why? The moment you see things falling into ruins simply means that you've changed your attitude on it. And the minute you change your attitude on it, everything crumbles. And if you hold the attitude here, it reformulates. Same energy. You know the same attitude that makes you sick, you know if you believe and live a life that is reckless, and if you hear the warnings that it is going to be devastating to your health, it always is. But that same energy that caused the sickness can release the destruction the moment the mind releases the focus on it. When the mind changes its mind, the energy falls apart and reconvenes as radiant health, the same energy. Do you understand? So be it.

Now P.S. Runners: I like them. And I do not send them as often as most people would like for me to. But they are my runners that come to teach you something about everything you've learned here. Always bless them, always. If someone is in your face and they are bawling you out, as you call it, and suddenly you realize what they are saying is true, start laughing. They're a runner. Don't slap them and trip them. Say, "What you say is true. Thank you for showing it to me." What does that do for an enemy? If you are going around kissing your enemy, you have disarmed them. When you start thanking them for their rudeness, there is no more enemy, is there? Do you understand? So be it.

Now the teaching today I want you to pay very close attention to and I want you to get involved with what you're learning. That way the learning will stay with you. And here's something you should know: You can never manifest anything unless you first have the knowledge about it. Got it? So be it.

# VI.

## The Auric Field

Have you heard the term auric field? Do you believe that you can tear an aura? Do you believe that? How can you tear energy? How can you rip up a thought? Auras, that is a metaphysical term for a band of energy that's actually dual, that surrounds all human beings.

We see that you have dual bands around the body. In other words, it's not just a gray aura or a blue aura or a rainbow aura. It's very specific about energy because an aura is levels of frequency with levels of consciousness. Now hold out your arms to your side. That's how wide the field is around your body. Now put both of your arms out, stretch them out and look at the distance of your field. Take a look around. Now go sideways and look at what is in your field.

This field, extending to the tips of your fingers, is actually a set of two bands. The first one ends here (the elbow), the second one ends here (the tips of the fingers), and it goes all the way around you.

The field cannot be seen with human eyes except for the field closest to the hand. If we were to put a black cloth on a wall and set two of you up in front of the wall and the rest of you to the back of the room and turned out the lights, except for a small light on, you would be able to see, literally, the first band in the lower frequency around the body around everyone that we put in front of that backdrop. You would actually see it. It is not a trick of the light; it's only what is visible to the brain. Got it?

**LIVING THE IMAGE**

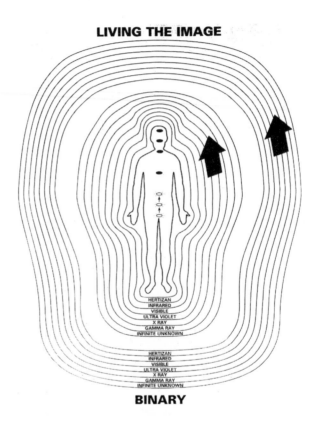

**BINARY**

Now take out the triad that we drew and set it beside the drawing with the bands. Do you remember when we were working with this triad and the seven levels? Remember we did it first with the hands and then with the drawing? Remember when we started, if you will recall, we talked about the energy between two points. And we said that's time. And you remember we talked about what happens to this energy when we slow it down to the next level. What happens to it? What happens to this energy if we bring it down into the first plane time field?

Now if we took this energy and slowed it down, it would wind itself up. It normally looks like undulating fields called the serpent. If we took this nucleus and brought it all the way down to the first plane, we would have what science finds baffling about life. What they are baffled about is subatomic fields, minute and atomic particles. You all know what an atom looks like. If we were to unravel an atom, starting with an electron and its positrons, with that which is termed the outward shield, we could actually unravel an atom starting on the first plane all the way up to the top of the triad and every part would equal one of those levels of time. Do you understand that?

So science is trying to understand life from the big to the little instead of understanding life from the little to the big. Do you understand? So what this means then is that all matter, including your body, is made out of or made up of atoms, and if you coagulate atoms together in what is termed a brotherhood, those atoms create gross matter. Gross matter then creates molecules. Molecules then create tissue.

So then if we were to take a microscopic cell out of your body, it would still be big compared to the subatomic field. Are you with me? So what does that tell you, my beautiful students? It says then that all life is made up of condensed Consciousness and Energy in the form of particles. And what science is endeavoring to understand is how these particles form a partnership. How does one atom know to connect and share electrons with another atom? How do they know that? In other words, what is the intelligence behind an atom?

For example, if everything you have in your body is made up of atoms, then why is your garment feeling different than your skin? I'm here to tell you that all atoms share a relationship together according to consciousness, and consciousness is the pattern that glues them together. Remember, energy is consciousness in motion. So even if we have energy, we have an inextricable riding field called consciousness. So every atom and every part of the atom, all the way to its orbit, has a mind. So every atomic structure is mind.

Now if we understand that it takes the entire triad to create an atom and that it takes time and mind to coagulate that atomic field, we can readily explain how everything got here on Earth. We have a free form of energy and we had a superior intelligence that focused a thought that became the lord of energy. And energy mutated and created the relationships and coagulated to fill in the pattern of thought. Are you still with me? Every tree, every insect, every grain of sand came from a superior intelligence. And sand is simply coagulated energy in the form of particles. But what holds it together is a mind, and the mind is what has put that atomic field into relationship with itself. It's attracting itself. Do you understand?

So then the large is made up of the invisible and the visible is made up of the invisible. In order to correct the visible, to make change on a geographic scale, even in your own reality, it's not about us going and cutting up these things. And it's not about us sweeping the sand out of our life. It is about changing our mind to the large structure. Then the large structure falls apart and *rerelationships*. It recoagulates itself to the new relationship and takes a new form.

Now where is this fast time? When Yeshua ben Joseph became the Christ, he was living in this time flow on this scale right here (fourth level). His body was made of all of the particles in this time flow (first level). Now his consciousness and his mind spent the rest of his life accelerating his mind up this scale, all the way up. So he was able to bring about the mind that flows in the upper kingdoms and also the consciousness that flows in the upper kingdoms. He was able to take that consciousness into his three-dimensional brain. So instead of thinking like a three-dimensional person, he thought like a seventh-dimensional God.

Now this kingdom right here (sixth level) looks vastly different than this heaven (fourth level). Why there are life forms that you can't even begin to imagine because you have no reference point. The only thing you can imagine is what is already set down here ( first level). The mind that it took to create the upper kingdom and its outrageousness and its unlimitedness and its eternalness is the same mind this entity developed down here in the lower kingdoms.

So look at how he saw life, will you? He knew that however he saw anything was exactly how he agreed for it to be. Are you with me? So when he saw the blind man and the blind man asked for help, he bent over and picked up some clay and he spat on it. Now what he was doing with the clay and his spit was creating a new biofield of particle relationship. And when he did this, he put it together and put it on the blind man's eyes. In molding the clay, Yeshua ben Joseph saw perfect vision. So as he was molding the clay, the clay became the catalyst to perfect vision. Are you with me? So when he put the clay to his eyes, that biofield, or morphogenic field, immediately reconstructed the visual nerve supply to the back of his brain and he saw instantly.

Now we call that a miracle worker. So how powerful is it to be like this entity who every day of his life worked up to this level of relationship with the particle field? What did he have to do? Walking down the path he would see and he would choose immediately whether to agree with the landscape or change it. So if he was walking and stirring up saffron dust, if he found delight with that, then he was agreeing with the dust. Are you with me? So then the dust would never change, would it? How many times do you walk down the path and stir up dust and are agitated with it? That only enforces its nature, doesn't it?

If he walked into a group of people and he is teaching them and then he stops to feed them — listen to me — and he only has a basket of fish and a loaf of bread and he has 5,000 people, what would your mind say? "Let's run to the market right away." But this is a master who understood the relationship between mind and matter, and all he had to do was to change his mind on what he saw. And so the fish and the bread became the seed that multiplied in his mind. And as long as he saw it, the supply was endless. Now where did the supply come from? The supply came from one fish and a loaf of bread, and all he needed to do was make them multudious. He kept creating echoes of the fish and the bread. And he was taking energy that was falling apart and recoagulating it, giving them a frame of reference in which to coagulate.

If you stop and think about it, someone told the rose to be a rose. Someone told it how to smell. Someone or something described to the rose, in a mental thought, deep, velvet red. Someone did that. Because it didn't just spring up on its own; it was created to be what it is. Not only the rose, but birds and water and environment. Someone focused them into evolution. Who was that? You, because it's what you expect. Do you understand?

Now Yeshua ben Joseph was considered a master all the way to the sixth level. He was only a master, not a Christ. And his job, as difficult as it was, was to defy reality with his mind. Look, I'm telling you today that what you think affects all life around you. Then if you stop for a moment and reflect, you will see how your life will stay static according to your imaged thoughts. You drive down the city, you expect to see the city; the city is there. You expect to see people begging; they're always there. You expect to see a car wreck on the side of the road because you need a little excitement. There's always one, isn't there? If that's true and you have the power, imagine what an initiation it was for such a being, and beings, that every day they had to defy physical reality and overlay with a mind so powerful that they could see what was not there and make it there. Powerful, eh?

You think that is more powerful than you? No. It is you. But where's your energy? Your energy is that you accept what is mundane in your life. You accept your ill health, you accept your problems, you accept your limitations, and because you accept them you freeze them and lock that energy into a relationship. That's what you do every day. You're a God and you are doing that. Imagine what it would be to get up every morning and to defy reality, to start changing what has been normal to you to be super-normal every day. So the first day you get up and a few things change, but not everything. Is that enough to get up and accept mundane reality? Or is it that we're having to create a mind that is so powerful that it can acquiesce the energy field of any life form and any situation and change it immediately. What does that take? Constant focus of what is expected rather than what is seen. How many of you got it?

# Some Insight from Quantum Mechanics

The study of quantum mechanics, quanta, means packets of energy. The mechanical activity of this energy is a noble science. It is gaining stronghold now back into the scientific community. And what is different in quantum mechanics than in Sir Isaac Newton's field of reality is that quantum mechanics says, like the scientist's experience, that whatever you think that a particle is going to be like, it always is. So they began to understand then that particle behavior had absolutely everything to do with the observer.

Imagine this for a moment. Imagine that a scientist is going to set up an experiment with life. And he draws a board and he draws a little slit. Let me show this; it is very comical. He's going to shoot light photons through to a board. This is the board; it's a negative. But here is an obstruction; it's a wall. And he has got his little photon machine right here. But what he's done is that he has cut a little tiny slit in the wall. So if he shoots the light out, it should go in a straight direction. And what he wants to see is that if light makes it through this barrier, it will show up as little dots on the negative on the board. So he turns the machine on and he shoots the ray of light out, and guess what the light does? It sneaks right down and hits the board. Well, that was pretty amazing. That light had a mind of its own. How did it know to do that? Then he said, "Well, we'll take care of this." So he plugs up the hole so now it can't get through. So he turns the light on and it just makes light bombardment onto the barrier wall.

So then he does another experiment. He gives it two options. So he makes the original slit again and one wee little slit at the bottom of the barrier. He turns the proton machine on again and half *go* through the upper slit and half go through the wee little slit at the bottom. Ah, amazing. How did it know to do that? Who's the observer observing the light particles? What did the scientist have in mind to do to the light? Wasn't he going to test it? But in his mind did he give the photons a way to get through? Since he did, then his mind is exactly what the light is going to do. The light knows to go through the slits because the scientist knows that they are there.

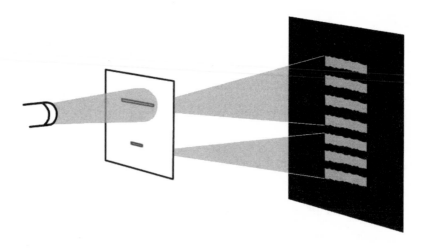

Now science calls this the "observer effect" so much to the point that they began to understand something else, which is important to understanding this. They have concluded that, for example, a hydrogen atom with its electron is in orbit because when they study them they see different trajectories around the nuclei. When they came to the realization that the observer is always affecting particles, then they came to the conclusion that there was no particle orbiting the atom but rather that it was an electron cloud. And they were correct. And do you know when they discovered the electron? When they expected to find it there. You like that?

So imagine what all these atoms are doing when we turn our backs. Imagine a pool table. You turn around and all of the balls are there. You turn your back and they fuzz out. The moment you turn to look at them, they're back to normal. That's the way that it is. How do you know the Earth is still around when you go to bed at night? How do you know you're here?

This is a great leap for science because, if that's correct, they have to make the next step and they have to say, "You are creating life." Now do they dare say that? Why they'd be burned at the stake or put in front of a firing squad. That's heresy. But it's true.

So if that's so, then the mind of the most humble man or woman is constantly holding form. Don't you know what a law is? A law says you have to obey the form and to break it is against the law. You're operating on a law of an agreement. You agree that this is the way that it is.

When Yeshua ben Joseph was moving his mind up to a lofty state and held it there, he was actually not of this world but indeed, as it's been said, he was in this world. His spiritual self was coming from the lofty kingdoms while his physical self remained here. And it wasn't until he got to the seventh level that he had to die — this is the ultimate test — that he had to agree to die, as the final initiation. What a final test. How do you defy death? First off you have to die. Otherwise it isn't a test, is it?

Now imagine how terrifying that is. None of you are at that place yet. But imagine how it would be to fully develop God on this plane. How would he do that? The final test would be that he would agree to die in front of everyone. And so powerful was his mind that he called it "the Father within me." The Father within him was the lower cerebellum that we all have. So powerful was he that he allowed the body to die and to go into decay. And then at the appropriate moment he was to reestablish a relationship with the body. Is that possible? Students, is that possible? Given what scientists say that we do with particles, is that possible? It is indeed.

So where is the loophole here? The loophole is that we are so terrified of life that we never live. We are so terrified of dying that we never live life. No one in this room has the capacity to do that because no one has built up such a wall of reality that "lay the body dead as it is, I will resurrect it." No one has developed that because they haven't lived yet. So imagine what kind of body he had then. The body went into physical corruption for three days and he came back.

What is it that came back? See the triad drawing that we did? When I told you yesterday that we were descending into involution to this present time line, that's true, we have. We all have an echo, meaning that we have contributed to the atmosphere as well as the mind on every one of the seven levels. So we already have a body existing on every one of the time frames. It is already there. It's hard to believe, isn't it?

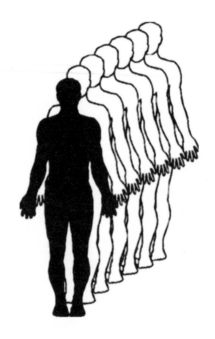

But we have a body here in the physical form, and we have a body on each of the other six levels. The body that we left behind is an echo. It's a mind; it's rolled up. It's rolled up waiting to be unrolled. The moment we access any one of these bodies, we do so by focusing equal to our level of acceptance, equal to one of these levels. And when we do, we start to unroll the atmosphere in that level and that becomes the stream of consciousness that moves into the brain through the back of the brain called the reptilian brain. It's a stream of mind and it moves right in through the back of the brain and activates the neocortices. And this place is so familiar when it is accessed, you will wonder how come you left it behind.

But the moment that you leave it, you will think it a dream because it has rolled back up into another atmosphere.

Every human being has seven bodies, and they are enfolded in this physical body and they radiate into what is called the auric field that extends to the tips of your fingers. All seven bodies are enfolded inside of the gross matter that makes up the physical incarnation you have now.

You have been living on this time line for ten and a half million years, and 455,000 years ago we had an abrupt change to this and we only developed that about 40,000 years ago. So all of the bodies have been on a wheel of incarnation in which the wheel never got any further than the third level.

Now what does that mean? That means that in every lifetime, in addition to the first three bodies, we have completely contained within us four additional radiant bodies. On death we are in the third body, and enfolded in the light body are those four other bodies, four other frequencies. Going to the light is not the end of the story; it's only a familiar place. Enfolded inside the light radiant body are yet four other bodies that access different levels of time. They are our vehicle to get there. Do you understand?

## The Light Body

In your last lifetime you never went any further than the light. At the light, before you came back to this incarnation, you reviewed your last life. The review took place in your light body. It reviewed, unfolded all of the energy and gave you a living screen to see what you did, who you were, what you accomplished, how you evolved, and what you didn't evolve. It just unrolled the energy and allowed it to play. Then once you had decided and made up your mind to come back, you were thinking with a light body, not a human body. But you were still cognizant that you could have done better in the physical body. Don't you find it interesting that entities who go to the light talk about viewing their life and that they viewed it with a cognitive judgment? They didn't have this brain. How could they make an opinion of what they saw? Because they did have a brain. What was the brain? It wasn't the gray tissue that sits up here, but it was a brain equal to the body they were inhabiting.

When you die you move immediately into infrared. It's the psychic realm. From the psychic realm the shaft of light appears and you go down it and you are actually moving from the low end to the high end of infrared, and then you hit the light. Who's the light? You. It's there that you view everything.

While you are making a decision about your physical life, there are four other potential lives or bodies that are enfolded in the light. And all you keep doing is agreeing to come back to this one.

So you've never changed those four other bodies. They are what we call hidden. We always change the light body, because the light body looks just like the body you are sitting in today, except younger and healthier. Why does it look like the body you have today? Because the body you have today couldn't look the way it looked unless it had a light field around it to give it the mind to be that way.

So we are always recycling the light body, the infrared body, and the physical body, but we have yet to use the hidden bodies of the upper four realms. Stay with me. I'm going to give you a lot of knowledge.

All of these bodies are in you and around you. If you look at your hand and you think about the atomic field that we just discussed earlier, think about this. The radiating field of one singular atom is equal to the radiating field of one of those bodies. In other words, every atom in your hand is the composite of seven levels of time. You got it? So the hand is a product of seven levels condensed to this. But what if we could defy that reality? What if we defied our body looking this way and insisted on it looking another way? Would it be possible to do that? Do you agree? Absolutely is.

You see, quantum mechanics doesn't say, "This works for the electrons but not for you." This field that surrounds your body has got within it the seven bodies hidden within your own tissue. When this dies, it gives up one body in the beginning; the one body is infrared. But in the infrared body is contained all the other bodies and you keep peeling them off.

So what does this have to do with Yeshua ben Joseph becoming a Christ? He had to prove that he was accessing the upper kingdom of God. And he had proved it every single way by all of the miracles and teachings that he imparted. But there was one thing that terrified all men in their hearts, and that was death. You see, the Hellenistic Jews of that time were the only ones that believed in reincarnation. The Jews of Abraham did not believe in reincarnation. They believed in hell, which was a terrifying aspect, which simply meant a shallow grave in which they would be dismembered.

Yeshua ben Joseph had to show to a culture of people that there was life after death. And the way that he had to do that was he had to sacrifice his own life. So he has to pull out this consciousness of the seventh level. And he had to let the body die and he had to move all the way, unfolding all those bodies all the way until he's at the top and he says, "My Father and I are one." He's saying that, "My mind is no longer from the House of David in these terrible times. My mind is my Father within me, who is the seventh level mind, the greatest mind." And he had to take off every one of those bodies, even the light body. He couldn't keep it on. He had to pull off the light body to manifest the blue body. He had to pull off the blue body, which is Shiva, and manifest the golden body. He had to pull off the golden body and go to the rose body, and then he had to go to infinite unknown. And only when he did that was he incorruptible.

And it was from this state that he resurrected his body and gave it life. What he gave it is eternal life. In other words, his physical body was vibrating nearly at the rate of light. And he only kept it slow so that he could interact with people and give them a last teaching. Why was this body radiating so fast? Because that was where his consciousness was. God now was man. And he lifted it up and reconstructed its physical matter, and he reconstructed it from the point of God so it was vibrating very fast. And when he left, where did he go? He simply kept raising the frequency. In other words, he started to spin his atoms around, and then the spin collapsed inward to the inside of the nucleus and it started spinning. And all the time he was doing that, the spin allowed every one of his particles to go into free space. So he was unfolding the seven bodies. And when he disappeared, he disappeared at light.

And that was when he was called the Christ, the Arisen One. That was the last test. That meant his consciousness had to be one with this so absolutely that not even death could defy that mind. And in doing so we now have great myth and legend and religion circling this entity.

But what has never been told to you is that it is not Jesus that's going to save your life but rather that he was a master who demonstrated the power of God in man, and if anyone had the eyes to see it, then they would understand. And if anyone had the ears to hear the message, they were offered the message and they had to be simple enough to understand the transmutation of the human Spirit into eternity, and it was demonstrated. And it wasn't demonstrated just with him. It has been demonstrated throughout the eons in every culture because people soon forget.

So what do we have now? We now have a religion around Jesus being the only son of God. That doesn't make any sense because everyone is the sons and daughters of God, not just him. And he can't save you. If he could, he would have saved you in the first century. You understand?

And how come he didn't teach his disciples this? Because they were simple men. They were fishermen. They were tax collectors. They were people just like you. How could he teach them that? He couldn't. All he could do is teach them in parables and in deeds. And he said, "Believe. If your eye lies to you, pluck it out. If you believe and your arm defies you, cut it off." That was an analogy to say no matter what your physical body does, it isn't the truth. Understand?

# VII.

## Kundalini and the Seven Seals

Every one of you has this same triad and the power that is not only around your body but is enfolded in your body. The human body with its brain and its seven centers — not chakras — are called seals. A chakra is where two lines of energy cross, and that's a chakra point. These centers are called the seven seals. Every one of you has them. They are equal to the triad drawing . And how simple is this? It means that what is important to you is where your energy will sit. How many of you in the audience think that the only thing that is important to you is your sexuality, procreation, your pain and suffering, and that's all that's important to you? You like to suffer and make people suffer. You are warlike creatures. Or you are powerful people. You are tyrants. You are tyrants and you are victims.

These attitudes have to do with the first three energy vortexes. They are called seals. And everyone has these open. What does this mean? It means that the first three bodies' energies are working on this three-dimensional Earth plane with its time flow. It's necessary to have these open in order to exist here. But these also are delivering energy every day. And whatsoever you think, the energy in your body opens.

And imagine as Yeshua ben Joseph was born from the first seal. He grew up going through his youth and having his first center activated, having his second center activated, and having, at his last test in the desert of forty days, his power being tested through abuse (third center). Now that's as far as anyone goes on this plane. That is not to demean intelligence. We can have a neocortex brilliant person, but their energy is only operating in the first three seals. Neocortex brilliance usually is in agreement with the establishment, so their energy is open in these first three seals only.

Let's think about Yeshua ben Joseph. In order for him to have healed a blind man, he had to have had energy not coming out of the first three seals, but that energy had to come from above these first three seals. He had to open up and develop and make manifest his fifth-level mind, the mind that exists in the upper kingdoms in order for him to perform a miracle here on the first plane. So what did that mean? That meant that in that moment all of his energy was sitting in his fifth seal, not in his first three seals.

Your body today has seven seals. The bands are the way that your physical body is held together, according to these seals. In every human being we have energy spiraling out of the first three centers. Now if that is what is pulsing out, then that energy is manifesting as sexuality, pain, or power. How many people do you affect with that attitude?

Now if we could take and unlock these upper seals, then we would activate these upper levels of awareness. If we did, then we could change all reality and bring about a lofty mind to recreate our reality.

I want you to explain the seven bodies, what they are, how many of them are activated at the present time, and how many of them stay hidden.

Now take your right hand and position it on your body where it is indicated on the drawing, and then I want you to read the description of each one of those seals, touching your body in that part, making contact with it.

# SEVEN SEALS* THAT CONSTITUTE SEVEN LEVELS OF CONSCIOUSNESS IN THE HUMAN BODY

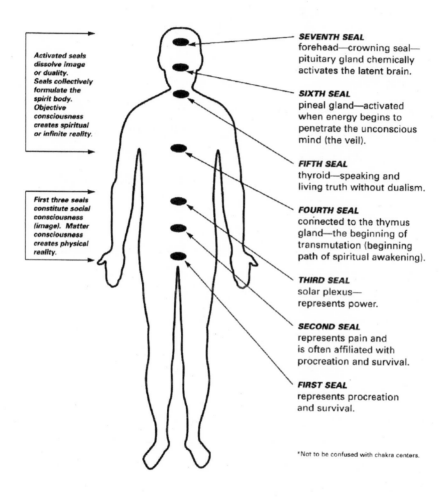

Activated seals dissolve image or duality. Seals collectively formulate the spirit body. Objective consciousness creates spiritual or infinite reality.

First three seals constitute social consciousness (image). Matter consciousness creates physical reality.

**SEVENTH SEAL**
forehead—crowning seal—pituitary gland chemically activates the latent brain.

**SIXTH SEAL**
pineal gland—activated when energy begins to penetrate the unconscious mind (the veil).

**FIFTH SEAL**
thyroid—speaking and living truth without dualism.

**FOURTH SEAL**
connected to the thymus gland—the beginning of transmutation (beginning path of spiritual awakening).

**THIRD SEAL**
solar plexus—represents power.

**SECOND SEAL**
represents pain and is often affiliated with procreation and survival.

**FIRST SEAL**
represents procreation and survival.

*Not to be confused with chakra centers.

I want you to take a red color and draw what looks like a sleeping serpent just underneath the first seal; a coiled, sleeping serpent.

Have you have heard of the term Kundalini? The Kundalini is an old term and an ancient law. It says that in every human being there lies the sleeping serpent or the sleeping dragon. It is the dragon or the serpent energy of life and it lies coiled in the base of the spine. Ancient teachings also say that when this serpent is aroused, some very extraordinary things happen. This energy is not the same energy that is responsible for the energy coming out of the first, second, and third seals. This is a large packet of quanta. It is something that is reserved for something very special, that's hidden and reserved for human evolution. It is said that when the serpent arises, it splits itself. And this serpent is sitting at the base of the spinal column that allows electrical information from all the nervous systems to be supplied to the entire body. So this spine and this energy are interested in this particular path. This path, from the base of the spine to the front of what is called the silent place in the neocortex, is called the journey. It's the journey of enlightenment, and it takes place when this serpent wakes up and starts to split and dance around the spine. It is powerful energy that is moving up and down the spinal column, ionizing the spinal fluid and changing its molecular structure. And as this serpent dances up the spine, it is changing the basic DNA pattern of the entire body. Moreover, the end of its journey means that the serpent's energy moves up into the midbrain.

The reptilian brain surrounds the upper brain stem in an area called the reticular formation. It looks like a mesh of webs. Now listen to me very carefully. The seat of the subconscious is not in the midbrain; it's in the reptilian brain. Moreover, this reticular formation, as you see on your drawing, is actually a trunk line of switches that allows certain information to flow and go on to the neocortex. This is a computer and whatever is programmed into it becomes reality, especially affecting the body. So when the serpent energy or the dragon energy of the Kundalini rises up the spinal column, it is ionizing with polarized energy the entire fluid that flows up and down the spinal column. When it hits the reticular formation, it opens up all of the switches. What does that mean? All of the doors to the subconscious are flung open. Further, the energy — like a dynamic conqueror marching, destroying, setting on fire everything in its path — is the march of the Kundalini.

When it comes to the midbrain section, there is an entity called the thalamus. In ancient terms it was called the "guardian at the door." And in myth and lore everyone thinks the guardian at the door is St. Peter, but it is not so. It is St. Thalamus.

The Kundalini energy activates this door to be open, and the thalamus is critical in the midbrain section because it is also the protector of the pineal gland. But the thalamus is where all the trunk lines from the nerve endings meet with all of the fibers from the reticular formation; it's a switching point. When the Kundalini opens this energy, everything that has been hidden from you in the form of the subconscious now flows freely to a specific point in the brain called the frontal lobe. Why is that so dramatic? Because the Kundalini opening up the switches and doorways, allowing ancient knowledge to come to the surface, is allowing the subconscious total access to your conscious mind.

We call the Kundalini a tribute to total enlightenment. Total enlightenment means that you get to peer beyond the veil to know what has never been known and you get to experience in a moment all that there is. In a flash of blinding light you can immediately see all the lives you have lived and all the lives you're going to live. And immediately it is all known. And how is that possible? The Kundalini energy, or the dragon force of the Near East, has been encoded. It was set there with rocket fuel to enlightenment.

Remember when I took you from the beginning point where you were created by the Void, and then you contemplated yourself and created the first level? You remember? Remember we fell all the way down to the first plane, three-dimensional reality? That's where you are right now. And I said to you that the consciousness of the human brain swings like a pendulum. It's supposed to in order to dream. There is a magic moment that happens, that even science now recognizes, that is in the swinging of the pendulum. There is a moment that it pauses. Now when it swings like a pendulum, it represents the polarity of thought: negative, positive, no, yes, lower, higher, dark, light, etc. Is there a moment when the movement of this hand is not going forward or not going backwards and is in that magical pause? Is there a moment that it's standing still? There is. It's the moment when both hands come right up in alignment. When you put both levels of consciousness in alignment like this, we call this the Eternal Now. It's the center of the magnet. At this moment there is a dynamic force of energy that is reflected from the mirror consciousness to the God. It's like in a tunnel. That tunnel energy is exactly what the Kundalini is.

Now this energy is rarely shaken from its slumber in human consciousness because most human beings have it shut down. Understand? In other words, to totally know, to totally be focused, to be totally unaware that you are human is a very rare moment. That only becomes when we have two levels of consciousness working: the observer and the doer. Got it? Now if we wake up and go into focus, the force field between these two is like a powerful magnet.

Now I'm telling you this in very simple and childlike terms. Whenever you dream a dream, it means that your consciousness has moved out; it's dreaming. When it's finished with a dream, it's supposed to move. In other words, it's a mirror. It's captured the drawing; correct? Its natural momentum is to line up with the observer. The pyramid is collapsing to Point Zero. That means that in order to affect reality we have to take the image back to God, the observer. So it closes up all time and we are in a no-place. We disappear for a moment. When the observer and the doer part, look what happens. We are pulling this vacuum, this energy, back down. What is important about this pull? What is important about it is that our dream is the new program, and we're pulling the energy down with a mental thought. So every one of our bodies, every atom in our body is reshuffled and reprogrammed according to this dream. Got it?

We are naturally supposed to dream and focus into the Now. Nothing else exists except this. When this is accomplished, it is this energy that is moving up the body and bringing about a state of euphoria. This euphoric state is when the dragon awakens, when the observer and the doer are in alignment with each other.

The serpent has now programmed the entire cellular structure and is now collapsing back into form. And the next moment reality is reformed. That's how it works.

Now you philosophically understand about the Kundalini. It is an energy that exists only in total alignment in the Now. That's the only time that energy exists.

Now how many of you recognize the caduceus? What does this symbol represent? Health. What does it look like? The staff looks like the spinal column and the orb on top is representative of the brain. There are two different serpents winding in complement to one another and then facing the orb. Looks like the Kundalini, doesn't it? What are the wings on the orb? What would the wings represent symbolically? Freedom. It is no accident that the caduceus represents absolute health in the medical profession, except they forgot what it means.

This sign in antiquity tells us that we can move into the Now with the focus of radiant health. And if we can hold the Now, this is exactly the story that happens and we are healed. The only way we are healed is to raise this energy by circling our spinal column, moving all the way up to our head, and in its journey ionizing the magnetic field that it's creating. It is changing the nucleonic spin of all the atoms that make up our body and is reshuffling the DNA.

Have you heard of people who healed themselves with their minds? This tells you how they did it.

# The Brain

I want you to read the names of the parts of the brain and associate yourself with each of the areas. It was once thought that the pineal gland was the seat of the soul. It is not the seat of the soul. It is St. Thalamus. Look at your drawing.

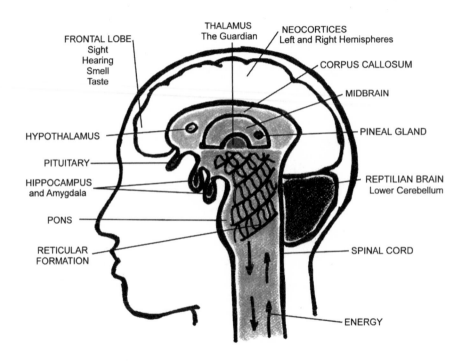

Now let's take a look at the brain now that you've familiarized yourself and mapped yourself with its parts.

We are going to talk about linear time as an arrow. Let's turn and look back on the arrow from whence it came. If we look in between ten and a half million years ago and 455,000 years ago, the human brain looked drastically different. We did not have that which is termed the amygdala. We had the hippocampus, but we did not have the frontal lobe, as we know it, or the neocortex. Prior to 455,000 years, the brain was very small. How many of you have seen the skulls of hominids of antiquity? Remember how small the back of the skull was? The back of the skull ended where the corpus callosum is. So all it had were the midbrain and the reptilian brain. That was prior to 455,000 years.

Now that is not a bad thing since this was the original brain. It is called the reptilian brain because they dated it to that which is termed the Reptilian era. It's been around that long. But do not confuse that with the brain of a reptile, although some people, it could be argued, have acted like that.

Let's use the arm as an example of the brain stem. The fist represents the midbrain section. The arm is the brain stem. And notice the reticular formation. Now take your other hand and wrap it very tightly around your wrist. The reptilian brain, or the lower cerebellum, has a very tight grip on the spinal column. In other words, all information coming from the brain to the body, all information coming from the body to the brain, is edited by this reptilian brain.

This fabulous hominid brain was much more spectacular than we've given it credit for. The human being itself looked vastly different than what you look today, especially in the cranium and the lower cranium. But this brain has been around since the beginning. We are carrying it with us through evolution. This is the brain which we accessed all levels of energy with when we were first in this body. The tissue of this reptilian brain is vastly different than the tissue of the neocortex. A tiny shaving of the lower cerebellum has more tissue, more atoms in one slice, than the entire neocortex put together.

So this grainy, darkly-colored organ is the transmitter and receiver of all the other levels. So the first hominid was actually receiving the intelligence of six other bodies, and we unfolded a stream of consciousness through that mechanism. The yellow brain, the neocortices, does not receive a stream of consciousness. That stream of consciousness only enters at the back of the brain. So we get new knowledge from the back door, the lower cerebellum, not from the neocortex.

This reptilian brain, up to 455,000 years ago, was our transmitter and receiver of the higher and multiplex dimensions from which we had just come. The midbrain section was intact and the pineal gland was much larger prior to 455,000 years ago than it is today. And if the reptilian brain is the seat of the subconscious, the midbrain itself is the seat of all psychic activity. It was created to be that way. The midbrain section is sensitive as a receiver to infrared radiation.

The midbrain section is the only part of the brain that is sensitive to infrared radiation. In other words, if you're occupying the Hertzian level at 8 Hz, the next level up from this (second level) is called the infrared realm. It is the realm you enter the moment you die. Infrared, as a band, has a low end and a high end band of its wavelength. This is what we have called the second plane of reality, very far from where we came. This band, because its wave is faster than the Hertzian band, is called the psychic realm. The hominids prior to 455,000 years ago were telepathic. They communicated much like the animals do today. Animals today are very telepathic creatures. Their brains are ultrasensitive to infrared radiation, and infrared is the psychic band.

So the hominids picked up and received thought through the band widths, as their brain was the perfect receiver. They picked up communication with the midbrain. The pineal gland, often called the soul of man, is responsible for manufacturing two neurotransmitters that are tantamount to consciousness in the yellow brain. One of these neurotransmitters is called serotonin. We call her Sara for short. Sara is a day girl. The pineal gland, when there is light, is producing serotonin. You can think of serotonin as a key.

Now the moment the light diminishes in the retina of the eyes, that contain the same cells that are located in the pineal gland, it signals the pineal gland to stop manufacturing Sara and start manufacturing Mel. Melatonin is the second neurotransmitter and melatonin is created to put the body to sleep.

So they configured that the off-and on -switch of human behavior was located in the head, and when they finally realized that it was the pineal gland they said, "Ah, that is the master switch." It is not.

However, it is the gland that we call the gland of the sixth seal. It is of tantamount importance. As soon as light penetrates your eyelids, which are transparent — and even if they're closed you still get light in — and the moment light starts to hit the retina, this gland produces serotonin. Serotonin is the "get-up-and get-going" neurotransmitter. It unlocks everybody that's asleep and turns them on.

Now the moment the light diminishes, as seen through the eyelids, the pineal gland switches and produces melatonin. It's the thing that makes you lazy and puts you to sleep. However, if the pineal gland is a little factory that manufactures these very important neurotransmitters, it does something else extraordinary: It synthesizes from melatonin a hallucinogenic drug called pinoline.

Now the shaman in the brain is the pineal gland. After midnight, at around 1:00 in the morning until about 3:00 in the morning, you move into your deepest level of sleep and your most lucid dreams occur there. Lucid dreaming is only possible if the pineal gland has had enough time to take melatonin and to change it into pinoline. Why pinoline? Pinoline is the hallucinogenic that the subconscious uses to allow the brain to communicate with the deeper spheres.

Now people who stay up late at night don't get to produce pinoline and therefore are robbed of this communication. That means that pinoline, distributed throughout the sleeping neocortex, reverse-fires the neurons and allows the subconscious mind to talk to the conscious mind. Thus pinoline opens the door to the subconscious mind and allows out-of-body experiences to occur. Furthermore, it allows prophetic vision to be seen on the time line and it allows you to move up into higher levels of consciousness. And before you return to your body, the pinoline is absorbed and you're back in your body.

The pineal gland produces serotonin and melatonin. And how about after midnight? Is there truth to the Cinderella story?

Now when the Kundalini rises and hits the pineal gland, it immediately, by virtue of its alignment and its energy, ionizes the spin ratio in the neurotransmitter serotonin. Now when we say ionizing the spin, what does that mean? Serotonin is a neurotransmitter molecule, and all molecules are made up of atoms. Do you agree?

Now the atoms that it takes to make a molecule called serotonin have all agreed to have an association and in that association their spins are relative to one another. They interchange electrons together, thereby changing mass, which in turn changes its chemical nature. So if there is a molecule of serotonin and then a hot wind of Kundalini, we have a powerful magnetic field of energy passing through this molecule. The energy is going to reverse-spin that molecule, thereby changing its characteristic. The molecule itself becomes fractured and is then reconfigured into its highest body, never its lower body. And the highest molecule potential of serotonin is pinoline.

And as this energy moves up into the midbrain and opens the door of St. Thalamus, the energy moves and starts firing simultaneously on the left and the right hemispheres of the brain. All the neurons start to fire. And with pinoline, immaculately changed in the twinkling of an eye, the brain is thereby capable of logging and registering time lines that go back to a point of eternity.

Now, my beautiful people, you have a little better understanding about what is sitting between your ears, eh?

The pituitary gland is the seventh seal. It's the crown because the pituitary gland directly affects the yellow brain and turns on all other glands starting from within the head to the rest of the body. The pituitary gland does this by secreting certain hormones that affects the pineal. The pineal then secretes its hormones and its neurotransmitters and turns on all of the rest of the glands going down into the body. If you were to have the pituitary removed, you would be dwarfed in your size and would not live for a great time.

In the beginning, prior to 455,000 years ago, this particular gland was mutated. In other words, it did not have the capacity that it does now. There was no need to have it then. So in the beginning stages of Homo erectus and his brain, he did not have a seventh seal. The seventh seal has become a graduated gland according to the use of energy.

The yellow brain came when the Gods came and took you as primitive entities and commingled their genes with yours, and it took from 455,000 years ago to 40,000 years ago to get seeded into the human DNA.

The first group of entities created from this cross-mutant were in the form of Mongolians. They were all olive-skinned and black-haired. Some carried an enormous amount of body hair. It would not be until 40,000 years ago, at the point where Cro-Magnon's brain was utterly fixed, that we have now a diversity of skin color, hair color, and eye color.

The large neocortex is exactly what the Gods have. Some of them have a larger neocortex than Cro-Magnon, but it is what they gave you. You have done little with it except use it automatically and genetically to operate your body, to operate your speech, to maintain balance, and use it for memory. You have used it in its barest form. But the majority of the neocortex lies unmapped. It lies unmapped because it's waiting for something to happen. It's waiting for a realization to occur.

And how does this realization transfer? The way that the brain is used in this school is that whatever sits in the frontal lobe becomes reality. The frontal lobe is the area above the eyes and the brow, called the quiet area in science. That is the area that all those who are adept at meditation focus on and the area that they tune into.

Whatever your brain puts there (frontal lobe) becomes law and as an observer will affect all energy fields, whether keeping it status quo or changing it. Now how does the brain do that? This yellow brain is created to fire holographic images; that's what thought is. And every neuron in your brain is hooked up to other neurons. Just to form the color yellow as a thought takes 10,000 and more neurons to fire simultaneously to give the color to a yellow sun.

The brain is used to make images, make them and create them. The brain is an imaging machine. The neocortices make images. Those images that sit in the frontal lobe are what preclude reality. They give reality. They allow reality. They either eternalize it or change it. And this is what science calls the observer.

When the scientist created the trick for the light and created a slit in the opening of the veil, he did that while he was thinking about it. That was his plan. He had a neuronet plan to follow. When he constructed the light to fall through, to be shown upon the veil, he knew there was a slit there. His brain fired the entire plan simultaneously. You call it thinking. But as the stream of thinking occurred, it was those thoughts about the plan that affected light and allowed light to move through the slit to the side of the negative screen. Again, whatever sits in thought is reality.

So the yellow brain is a great architect. Its job is to design archetypes. Its job is to think coherently. Its job is to provide you, the Spirit, with as great an amount of imagery as possible, because without it we don't collapse the wave into a particle form. Got it?

## Thinking about Thinking

Now think about this for a moment. What if you were conscious every day of your thoughts? Most of you are unconscious of your thoughts. You are unconscious of the way you speak. You speak like barbarians, like trash, unbecoming to Gods. You don't even use your words as force.

But what if, for a solid week, you were observing the way you thought. What if you got to do that? You would certainly see how a train of thought is the image that is necessary for creating life the way you've been experiencing it. So what if we change the picture? If we change the picture, we change reality. It's as simple as that. So the great runner I'm going to send you is to make you very conscious of your thinking for a week. So be it.

When I said to you, "Go and think of three things you would like," what did I tell you to do? I said think. So you're sitting there and you're telling your brain, "Now pull up the files. What do we want? Want, want, want. Let's see. What do we want? Oh." Your brain is forming thoughts. At first you had something and then you're trying to think of two more things. You are trying to think what you want. Isn't it interesting that you have to try to think of what you want? Why, if a genie appeared in front of you, you'd be tongue-tied for the first five minutes. You can have anything that you want. It's always safe to say, "If I can have anything I want, then everything I wish for after this I want because that's the only thing I can think of this moment."

The brain is giving you images. When you decided what you wanted, you had to make your yellow brain be creative with you. And then it would give you an image. And then you know what you did? You thought about the image. You know what else you did? You judged the image. "Oh, that will never happen. I don't deserve it. Oh, that's too much. Get real." That's what I'm trying to tell you to do; get real. You put up an image and then you analyzed it. Did you do that? Did you analyze what you wanted?

What if you just created something and didn't judge it at all and said, "This is what I want." What would happen? Would you get it? Do you think you would? What would happen if you judged it? What if you were running an analysis on this hologram, what would happen? You don't get it. You know why? Because it's under analysis. Even though it's sitting there, it's not permitted to do anything because it's being judged and weighed. It's being thought about, talked about. It's never left alone. As long as it's under analysis, it never manifests.

So think of the yellow brain as an archetype, a deliverer of images, and it puts it right in the frontal lobe. And from the backdoor in your brain the energy comes through the Kundalini to give it total credibility. Without energy it doesn't go anywhere. If we allow it, we give it the greatest energy of all. If we discern it, we take away from it; we limit its energy.

Have you learned? Are you older and wiser than you were yesterday?

So be it. Now here is what is very happy about this knowledge. When you truly understand how your brain works, how it affects energy and reality, it should become apparent to you that if it works for one thing it can work for everything. There is no law written anywhere that prohibits the use of that which is hidden in any area. You create everything. There is nothing impossible when you learn the science, when you learn the discipline. What sadly some people do is that they never apply it; they're too lazy. But it works. And if you can manifest a feather, you can manifest the ability to be Christ because it is the same energy across the board.

I love you greatly. That is all.

# VIII.
## Epilogue

I greet the God within you. Pray let us never forget where it is. Let's have a drink.

O my beloved God,
I do decree
That that which I focus upon
I surely want.
Manifest it straightaway.
So be it.
To life.

All that I have taught you will culminate into the pouring forth of that which is termed the substantialness of yourself, the God. All that I have told you will focus into a crystal truth when what you have created manifests. And if you are a charmed entity indeed, you are never going to forget this day nor what you have learned. And you will fall in love with magic and with God. And perhaps for the first time in your life you'll wake up and realize what you've been missing. There is nothing you cannot do. There is nothing impossible to you.

If you have the mind and if you have the brain to create an image and you have the strength to hold it in spite of all outward reality, you'll get it every time. All of those great Gods that came along 455,000 years ago came this way. And they already knew this science way back then. They have evolved on the evolutionary scale. They're in a different kingdom, in a different life, possessing different bodies, with a great deal of longevity to their life. Some lived thousands of years without dying; that's your right. You're now coming to a place of understanding that they once came. All that I have taught you works. If it were not so, all of these people that have belonged to this school for so many years would not keep coming back.

And if God does live within you, then most certainly with this extraordinary amount of lengthy words that were brought forth these two days, and all the writing and all the talking that you did, surely we have pinpointed the source of your divinity: Consciousness and Energy create the nature of reality.

The lists you made of what you wanted to change and what you wanted to have manifested in your life, I want you to put the date and your calendar year on those lists. I want you to put them in a place that you see them every morning and every night. And as they manifest in your life, I want you to write down the day and the date that the manifestation came into fruition because the only way you're ever going to believe in everything I've taught you is for you to experience it for yourself.

In the meantime, remember me when the wind blows. Think of me when your runners come. And never ever doubt that God lives within you ever again. Love I you greatly, masters. I am Ramtha the Enlightened One. So be it. That is all.

# Other Ramtha Titles

The following is a list of additional books on Ramtha available through Ramtha's School of Enlightenment and other fine book stores. Also available is a whole library of recordings and videos of Ramtha's teachings. All products are available through mail order at:

Ramtha's School of Enlightenment
PO Box 519
Yelm, Washington 98597
(800) 347-0439 or (360) 458-4771
email: greg@ramtha.com
Website: www.ramtha.com

RAMTHA *Edited by Stephen Lee Weinberg (217 pages).* The classic work on Ramtha, that Ramtha himself has referred to as "The Great White Book." A brilliant work designed to inform the general public as to the nature of Ramtha's teachings along with a rich sampling of his wisdom on many topics. Highly recommended for those ready to understand this great teacher and his message. It is one of the most important books to read if you are preparing to enter the school.

| | |
|---|---|
| #1401 - HardCover | $ 19.95 |
| #1401 - SoftCover | $ 12.50 |
| #1401 - Leather-Bound Edition | $ 29.95 |

RAMTHA: AN INTRODUCTION *Edited by Stephen Lee Weinberg (228 pages).* An engaging collection of teachings that will appeal equally to those familiar or unfamiliar with Ramtha. More than an introduction; a true treasure of personal mastery.

| | |
|---|---|
| #1404 - SoftCover | $ 9.95 |

I AM RAMTHA *Edited by Richard Cohn, Cindy Black, and Greg Simmons. (127 pages).* This book is a beautifully photographed book that accompanies thirteen of Ramtha's most universal teachings. Wonderful teachings on the subject of feelings, being at one with nature, unconditional love, and the prize that is called life.

| | |
|---|---|
| #1201 - HardCover | $ 9.95 |

THE ANCIENT SCHOOLS OF WISDOM *Compiled by Diane Munoz (172 pages)* is a teaching and introduction to the formation of Ramtha's School of Enlightenment. Ramtha tells the history of how the ancient schools operated in times past and why their instruction was so precious: to awaken the forgotten God within.
#7100 - SoftCover                                                    $19.95

A STATE OF MIND *JZ Knight (445 pages)*. The intimate account of JZ's life in her own words. Her story, which includes her humorous and poignant introduction to Ramtha, is a story of the triumph of the human Spirit. Also available in an edited audio version, recorded in her own voice.
#1501 - HardCover                                                    $ 9.95
#1501.1 - Cassette (120 minutes)                                     $ 9.95

TO LIFE *Compiled by Diane Munoz*. At the beginning of each audience, Ramtha elegantly and thought-provokingly salutes the God within with a toast. This book is a selection of the toasts from Ramtha's audiences from May 1988 through May 1996. A wonderful way to start your day!
#7101 - SoftCover
$15.95

CHANGE: THE DAYS TO COME *Ramtha (149 pages)*. Based on the 3-day intensive taught in Denver, May 1986. This book tells of man's destruction of Earth's resources and nature's recourse to heal herself. This book has never been more timely than now.
#1402 - SoftCover                                                    $10.00

LAST WALTZ OF THE TYRANTS *Edited by Judy Pope Koteen (153 pages)*. This book is a synthesis of Ramtha's teachings on the challenges we face by those who control the world economy and from the coming radical changes in nature. It provides inspiration and practical guidelines to enable you to be prepared.
#1202 - SoftCover                                                    $ 7.95

MANIFESTING: A MASTER'S MANUAL *Edited by Khit Harding (100 pages)*. Based on the November 1986 intensive, The Power To Manifest, this is compiled such that each page serves as a thought-provoking concept for contemplation and understanding.
#1102 - SoftCover                                                    $ 9.95

SOULMATES: THE INTENSIVE *Ramtha (128 pages)*. Based on the 3-day intensive taught by Ramtha in Seattle, WA, January 1986, this book spells out the mystery of the science of soulmates and its importance in knowing and loving self.
#1403 - SoftCover                                                    $10.00

SPINNER OF TALES *Compiled by Deborah Kerins (228 pages)*. Ramtha has captivated audiences throughout the years with his telling of tales. Now they have been put together in book form to be preserved and delight readers of all ages. These stories are from the earliest years of the teachings to the most recent. A true treasure!
#1300 - SoftCover                                                    $10.00

UFO'S AND THE NATURE OF REALITY *Edited by Judy Pope Koteen (221 pages)*. This book is a sometimes shocking, sometimes comforting picture of what we would call alien intervention in our history, in our present, and in our future. It allows us to see what is "out there." But this is more than another UFO book. It exposes the limitations of subjective mind and encourages the reader to move into interdimensional mind, the source from which all is available. This book will alter the way you've perceived everything you've been told.
#1611 - SoftCover                                                    $11.00

# Foreign Language Products

We have a large selection of Ramtha books in German and Spanish, a smaller selection in Italian, Japanese, and French. We also carry audio cassettes and videos in German and Spanish.

If you are interested in knowing more about Ramtha's School of Enlightenment, for a free introductory brochure and a cassette tape on The Ancient Schools of Wisdom, call or write to:

Ramtha's School of Enlightenment
PO Box 1210
Yelm, WA 98597
(360) 458-5201, ext.10
email: michele@ramtha.com